They're Playing My Song!

by

Rev. Ian W. F. Hamilton

A collection of short stories and talks many of which were originally
published in "The People's Friend" or broadcast on Grampian Television

Every Blessing

i

First published 1996
© Ian W. F. Hamilton 1996
ISBN 1 807151 06 2

Printed and Published by
MORAVIAN PRESS LTD.
31 South Street, Elgin, Moray
1996

To the memory of MARY and FINLAY HILL,
dearly loved grandparents.

THE AUTHOR

The Reverend Ian William Finlay Hamilton is Minister at Nairn Old Parish Church in the Highlands of Scotland, one of the largest congregations within the Church of Scotland.

Outwith his family and his ministry Ian's main interest is music — he has been playing the piano since the age of three and has studied music seriously in his earlier years. Part of his studies were undertaken as a part-time student at The Royal Scottish Academy of Music in Glasgow, his home town. In addition to his qualifications in theology Ian holds piano diplomas from two of the London Music Colleges. He also enjoys playing the church organ and in recent years he has produced a Piano/Organ cassette tape which features some of the music he most likes to play.

Ian Hamilton is a regular contributor to the media, and although he regards this as a hobby — and as a privilege — he very much sees this as part of his wider ministry through which he is given the opportunity to use his God-given gifts to help communicate the good news of the gospel.

He is a member of the team of Ministers who regularly present the week-night "Reflections" programme on Grampian Television, and included in this publication are the scripts from some of these programmes reproduced in and adapted for book form.

Additionally he has in recent years been a regular contributor to the "Manse Window" feature in "The People's Friend" magazine which has a weekly readership of approximately one and a half million! "I never cease to be amazed at the response that I receive from readers of "The People's Friend" — I get kindly and complimentary letters from all over the world!" Ian exclaims. Several of these "Friend" articles feature in this publication together with a selection of stories which have not been previously published.

Married to Margaret in 1971, the Hamiltons celebrated their Silver Wedding Anniversary in September of this year (1996) and sharing in these celebrations not least were their three children, David who is seventeen, and twins Gillian and Jennifer who are fourteen.

The Hamilton family headed once again across "the pond" for New Jersey in the summer of 1996 to participate in their fifth Summer Pulpit Exchange to the U.S.A.

The author's first two books, "Reflections from the Manse Window" (1992) and "Second Thoughts" (1994) — both published by Moravian Press — have been widely read and much appreciated.

FOREWORD

by

Rev. Dr. Willis A. Jones

formerly Minister at
WYCKOFF REFORMED CHURCH, WYCKOFF, NEW JERSEY

A contemporary wag has penned, "The question is not can you sing a song, but rather do you have a song to sing?" An ancient chorister in his own time and place was heard to lament, "How can we sing the Lord's song in a foreign land?" (Psalm 137).

Along comes the clerical minstrel Ian Hamilton disclosing that he most certainly has a song to sing, and he croons it in his own genial, kindly and loquacious idiom.

"REFLECTIONS FROM THE MANSE WINDOW" proved to be a popular collection of observations and inspirations somewhat reminiscent of the prophet Habakkuk scaling the skyscraper and peering into the meanings of the moment and the yearnings of the years.

"SECOND THOUGHTS" followed bubbling with chatty information and earthy thought-provoking gems. The books are targeted for "dear hearts and gentle people" and Ian's words, wit and wisdom bring a smile to the face and a lullaby to the soul. His style harks us back to a safer, a slower and a more neighbourly time when people could feel the freedom to be human.

Many will be on the tip-toe of expectation as Ian makes it a trilogy with "THEY'RE PLAYING MY SONG!" As one who has been frequently on the receiving end of Ian's humorous escapades and symphonic safaris, I greet with eagerness in this world of dissonance the happy harmonies of Ian's composing. Ian reflects an at homeness with those for whom he writes and an ease of style in his delivery, all coupled with a song well worth singing and pleasurably received.

Carry on Maestro, the audience is hushed, and we await . . . .

Willis a. Jones

Minister at Currie Kirk, by Edinburgh

v

ACKNOWLEDGEMENTS

Much of the material published in this book is based on articles which were written for and published in "The People's Friend" and the five "Reflections" series were originally presented by the author on Grampian Television.

Grateful thanks is expressed to D.C. THOMSON & CO. LTD., and to GRAMPIAN TELEVISION P.L.C. for concurring in the reproduction of the relevant material in book form.

The drawing on page 16 is reproduced by kind permission of Dr. Bea Card Kettlewood, Pompton Plains, New Jersey, to whom is expressed warmest thanks.

The drawing of the Ardclach Bell Tower on page 50 and the photograph on page 22 are reproduced by courtesy of D.C. Thomson and Co. Ltd.

Photograph on page 53 by courtesy of N.C.H. Action for Children.

Illustration on page 81 by Evelyn Pottie, Broombank, Loch Flemington.

CONTENTS

"They're Playing My Song!"

by

Rev. Ian W. F. Hamilton

"They're playing my song!"

ALL of us rather enjoy having the occasional compliment paid to us from time to time but recently one was paid to yours truly which rendered me almost speechless — "Impossible!" I hear many of you saying, but absolutely true I assure you!

The compliment was paid to me by my dear friend Bill Devlin who is a very competent church organist. Bill has served his church and his Lord in this capacity for many, many years (without giving his age away!) Originally from Glasgow, where he began playing the organ in the city's former Wilton Church, Bill and his dear wife Flora now live in Inverness and he is much in demand to play at services and church events. In fact he played the Nairn Old organ for our B.B.C. "Songs of Praise" broadcast a few years ago and he often deputises for us when our regular organist is unavailable.

Additionally Bill and I recently gave a joint organ concert here in Nairn — we called it "Seated one night at the Organ", a concert programme which contained all the "old favourites". Bill played his favourites, like "Prelude on The Londonderry Air", "Evensong" and "Angels guard thee" and I played some of mine, including "On wings of Song", "Sanctuary of the Heart" and the "Processional from The Sound of Music".

But not only is Bill Devlin a fine organist, he is a very keen and gifted composer of hymn tunes. In fact in recent years he has written several hymn tunes and set these to familiar hymn words. In addition to writing these tunes, he has kindly named them after several of the churches in the Nairn-Inverness area in which he has played. Bill has now built up quite a catalogue of original hymn compositions and they are appreciated and sung by many congregations.

Bill always gives me a copy of each new hymn tune "hot off the press" and recently when he was with us playing at our morning service he said to me following the worship, "Ian come over to the organ, I want to let you hear my latest composition". I listened with great interest as ever to the most marvellous tune, one especially rich in harmony and majestic in mood. "That's another winner Bill" I assured him. "Yes, I hope so" he responded, "and it's for YOU Ian!" It was when I looked at the NAME he had given his new tune that I was rendered almost speechless — he had called it "REV. IAN W. F. HAMILTON". "Bill, what a compliment

— many, many thanks!" was all I could struggle to say as emotion rather overtook me! Once I had regained my composure I added, "Now Bill I'll be one of the few who can truly say 'They're playing my song!'"

Bill Devlin at the Nairn Old organ console.

It is beyond doubt the nicest compliment I have ever been paid — I will treasure it forever AND I will make sure this super tune is sung, if not EVERY Sunday, certainly on a regular basis!

But of course the words to which hymns tunes are set are of equal importance, and the words Bill had chosen couldn't have been more suitable to complement his fine tune. He chose the words of "O Jesus I have promised to serve thee to the end" — a hymn of dedication and discipleship.

All of us who profess the Christian faith have promised to serve and follow our Lord as we live out our lives, to be his faithful disciples in the world today. And part and parcel of this "discipleship" we have promised, I have no doubt whatsoever, is to use to the very full the gifts and talents our God has given us in order to build up his church and to proclaim his message.

In the Church throughout the world there are good folks like Bill Devlin who week in, week out are graciously using their God-given gifts to proclaim in music and in praise, the message of the Master, and those of us who benefit from their talents and from their services thank God for them with all our hearts.

"What on earth shall I do?"

I had the strangest experience recently as I made my way by car from Nairn down to Glasgow. The journey most of the way south had gone fine — without a hitch! But as I came into the outskirts of Glasgow I encountered my first set of traffic lights — and I couldn't believe my eyes — they were showing both red AND green at the same time!

"What on earth shall I do?" I thought as I sat there with countless vehicles on my tail! I concluded hastily that all I could do was to look in every direction to ensure that there was no other traffic moving and then carefully negotiate the rather confusing traffic signals I had encountered.

But the question "What shall I do?" is as old as life itself — I'm sure many of you have often addressed it either to yourself or to someone else!

Sometimes we ask it calmly when a problem confronts us — one which demands careful consideration and action — like the faulty traffic lights on the outskirts of Glasgow! Sometimes we ask the question when we're gripped by fear or by distress. On the other hand there are times when we find ourselves in a situation where we have to decide clearly between two courses of action. Maybe the issue isn't very simple and clear-cut, and so in our uncertainty we ask "What shall I do?"

The question has been posed since the beginning of time, and it's one which is asked COUNTLESS times in the Bible! Indeed it was one that people often put to Jesus himself — and he never failed to provide them with an answer!

Perhaps you'll remember the wonderful Bible story of a man called Saul who had been determined to stamp out the new religion called Christianity which had sprung up so rapidly and which was winning so many people over to its cause. That was until Saul too made a journey one day down a certain road and met a strange experience, which in fact for him became a life-changing encounter! "This is what happened," as Saul himself describes the experience. "I was on the road to Damascus when suddenly a great light flashed from the sky. Then I heard a voice saying to me 'Saul — why do you persecute me?' I answered — 'Tell me who you are Lord.' 'I am Jesus of Nazareth whom you are persecuting' . . . . and I said . . . . 'WHAT SHALL I DO?' "

Well, as many of you will know, Jesus told Saul of Tarsus what to do — Jesus gave him direction — and in consequence, as Paul the Apostle, this man became the greatest ambassador of the new faith.

There are many of course who will pass through life and who will never have an experience as dramatic as that — nevertheless Jesus Christ comes to meet us as we walk life's road in many ways and often in the most unlikely situations!

Our response must surely be to allow Him to give us direction, to let Him journey along with us, and to give Him the joy of welcoming us when we reach our final destination!

 **MORAY ▪ FIRTH ▪ RADIO**

A Broadcast on the Cheep!

F ROM time to time I have the privilege of presenting each morning a programme called "Time for Thought" on the local radio station. It runs from Sunday to Friday and each time I do it I always try to have a particular theme running through the daily "God-slots".

It was suggested that I might present the last series I did with the help of my piano! And so, after great deliberation I eventually decided to play six film themes and offer a two-minute devotional thought on each of them.

The music of course had to be recorded at home and in order to do this the radio station had provided me with the necessary special recording equipment. All I needed now was some peace and quiet in the manse — not always a readily available commodity I assure you!

I opted to do my piano "takes" during the day while the children were at school in order to eliminate at least one source of possible interruption! With the telephone switched through to the church office for the short duration of the six takes and with Margaret my wife dutifully guarding the front door (lest I was beaten by the bell!) I proceeded to play. Happily all the film themes went well — without the proverbial hitch — at least SO I THOUGHT!

A few days later off I drove in to the studios in Inverness to record the "voice-overs." The idea was that I would put on the headphones and after hearing so many seconds of music I would be given a cue to start speaking. When the piano tape started to roll I couldn't believe my ears! "Is that BIRDS I hear there Ian?" asked the producer! It certainly was! Each piece of piano music was "accompanied" by the chirping and cheeping of birds outside the manse music room window! The radio station's equipment was extremely sensitive, so much so that it enabled my feathered friends which frequent the manse rose bushes to get into the act!

Of course re-takes had to be done — at dead of midnight needless to say!

I began the week by playing the theme music from the film "Exodus" — which had seemed appropriate with its Old Testament connotations, and I brought the "God-slots" to a close on the Friday with the beautiful theme from the film, "Love Story". That too I thought was appropriate, as the greatest love story ever told is to be found in the pages of the New Testament — the story of Jesus and his love!

But the wonderful thing about THIS love story is that it is endless — it goes on and on. Jesus' love is forever — for all God's children — and for all God's creatures . . . . EVEN THE BIRDS — bless them!

A church made of matches!

VERY often I take something into the pulpit with me on a Sunday morning to show the boys and girls — a kind of visual aid to help illustrate the story I have prepared for them. On a recent Sunday morning I had the most remarkable visual aid imaginable with me!

"What would you say boys and girls if I told you I had the Parish Church with me up here in the pulpit this morning?" I asked the children. They were very soon to realise that I **had** the Parish church with me — at least I had hidden in the pulpit the most marvellous model of Nairn Old Parish Church — a model made of matches by our Fund Raising Convener, Arthur Clark. "Isn't this wonderful boys and girls, and look at the detail that Mr. Clark has managed to include in his matchstick model!" The detail is superb in fact, from the intricate design around the 100 foot tower to the stained glass windows. Yes, Arthur had even managed to install imitation stained glass to represent Nairn Old's real and very beautiful stained glass windows!

Arthur Clark and some B.B. Anchor Boys admire the matchstick church.

7

Additionally Arthur had made the model church with a slot in the top and a "way in" underneath, which means that it can be used to collect gifts of money. "He's not the Fund Raising Convener for nothing boys and girls!" — at which point the congregation burst into laughter!

In fact our beautiful building celebrates its centenary in two years time and when the Centenary Appeal is launched very shortly, Arthur's model masterpiece, which took nine months to make, will be used to help gather in funds which will be necessary to celebrate that very important and significant birthday.

Unfortunately I can't disclose the number of matches Arthur used because it's a secret — Arthur knows and I know — and at present, the boys and girls in the Sunday School are playing a guessing game each Sunday! The answer is in a sealed envelope up there in the Nairn Old pulpit and there will be a prize for the one who gives me the correct answer — to the last match of course!

The matchstick model kirk.

After I had let the children see this most remarkable visual aid I went on to ask them how the matches in Mr. Clark's church were held together. "Glue!" they all said. "Yes, that's right boys and girls, and without the glue, Nairn Old Parish Church would come tumbling down — at least this version of it would!"

8

I then went on to ask them what held our REAL church building together. "What holds the bricks and the stones together?" to which they all replied in unison, "Cement!" "Right again boys and girls, and without that cement, which has become harder and harder over the last 98 years or so, the real Parish Church wouldn't stand up for long either!"

But of course, important and necessary as buildings are, I then went on to explain to the children that the church is much more than a building. The Church is really made up of PEOPLE. "All of US are Nairn Old Parish Church. This lovely building wouldn't be of much significance unless there were people to come along to it week after week and USE it for worshipping and praising God, as we all do!"

And our "Church made of PEOPLE" must be held together too. As the glue supports the matches and binds THEM to each other, and as the cement supports all the bricks and stones, the PEOPLE of the Church must support each other too. The best way of doing that, I told the Sunday School children — and the large congregation — is to follow the commandment of Jesus, namely to "love one another".

The thing that should bind the living church together is love, and I then quoted the words of a contemporary hymn, which runs like this:—

"Bind us together Lord, bind us together
With cords that cannot be broken.
Bind us together Lord, bind us together Lord,
BIND US TOGETHER IN LOVE."

And of course it is so very true, LOVE is the thing that should help all Christian people support one another, so that they may STAND FIRMLY TOGETHER in the service of Jesus!

GRAMPIAN TELEVISION

SOME "REFLECTIONS" . . . .

MONDAY

(Cue Ian at piano . . . . 35 seconds of "Dream")

Nice to be with you again!

"Dream when the day is through, dream and they might come true" . . . . sometimes they do and sometimes they don't!

There was once an M.P. who dreamed that he was making a speech on the floor of the House of Commons, and when he awoke, he discovered that he was!

Dreaming is a universal experience . . . . either an escape from, or a step towards reality. Most great achievements, in science, education, religion, whatever, were initially perceived as pictures in human imagination . . . . the stuff of which DREAMS are made.

William Booth just couldn't sleep one night so he decided to take a walk through the streets of London, and there, in the wee small hours, he witnessed poverty in the extreme . . . . people sleeping rough in doorways, under bridges, wherever, to shelter from the rain and exposure (many still do alas.)

When Booth got home he said to his wife, "I've been to hell." But out of his nightmarish experience, Booth's dream of The Salvation Army began to germinate . . . . a dream that became a reality!

"Dream when the day is through (or whenever) — dream and they might just come true!"

A very good and peaceful night . . . . and SWEET DREAMS!

(Ian plays out with a further 20 seconds of the song "Dream")

TUESDAY

(Cue Ian at piano . . . . 35 seconds of "Island of Dreams")

"Island of Dreams" by the Springfields . . . . I'm just young enough to remember them!

Dreams are often an escape from reality, especially perhaps when we're up against it, when things aren't going as well as we would like. Oh to escape . . . . even just for a few days . . . . to be miraculously transported far, far away to an island of dreams, where the sun is always shining and the sky is always blue! DON'T YOU BELIEVE IT!

And of course, you don't! Because even if this kind of dream was to come true, sooner or later we've got to come back to reality. Despite our present predicament, despite our yearning for a better lot than we may have right now, perhaps we'd do well to recall some words from a letter written long ago.

The man who wrote these words was up against it to say the least at the time of writing, nevertheless Paul the Apostle was able to say, "I have learned, in whatever state I am, therewith to be CONTENT."

A good and peaceful night . . . . and of course SWEET DREAMS!

(Ian plays out with a further 25 seconds of "Island of Dreams")

WEDNESDAY

(Cue Ian at piano . . . . 30 seconds of "I Have Dreamed")

Hello again . . . . "I Have Dreamed" from "The King and I" — a marvellous musical! And THAT we all certainly have done — we all dream dreams. But very often they turn out to be broken dreams . . . . as our national bard once put it; "The best laid schemes o' mice and men gang aft aglay."

So often the dreams we HAVE just never materialise — the harsh realities of life get in the way — sudden illness — redundancy — problems within our family. Indeed perhaps you've dreamed GREAT dreams for your children — maybe you had high aspirations for them, but things just haven't turned out as you had hoped. Dreams become broken, shattered sometimes.

How suddenly — and often how tragically — high hopes for the future can be turned upside down, totally reversed, into sad history.

So does this mean we shouldn't go on dreaming, hoping? Thomas Jefferson once said: "I like the dreams of the FUTURE better than the history of the past."

GO ON HOPING . . . . and go on having your DREAMS in the knowledge also that the KING . . . . not the one in the musical . . . . the OTHER King who gives us our hopes and dreams . . . . is more than able, if necessary, to help mend the broken ones — as countless folks will readily testify . . . . and . . . . SWEET DREAMS!

(Ian plays out with a further 20 seconds of "I Have Dreamed")

THURSDAY

(Cue Ian at piano . . . . 25 seconds of "Forgotten Dreams")

"Forgotten Dreams" — a classic, by Leroy Anderson, and yes some dreams we remember — vividly — but MANY we forget. And just occasionally there's a dream realised to a person that, in the fullness of time or in the light of experience or maturity, he or she WANTS to forget.

Once upon a time (that's a good start to any story!) there was a young girl in Toulon, very bright, very charming, with a wonderful singing voice . . . . AND she was a dreamer!

11

Left as an orphan she tried to make ends meet by singing in cafés — singing so well that she even dreamed of "making it" in Paris . . . . and she did! She captivated Paris and wealth flowed into her hands. Her dream had come true — known as Eve Lavallière she was rich and famous.

But suddenly she vanished — Paris searched everywhere for her, but to no avail. Eventually however, someone came across a woman, a poor woman working among poor people in a French mountain village. She was nursing the sick and scrubbing floors, singing as she scrubbed . . . . and yes, she was Eve Lavallière.

"Come back!" Paris begged. "No" she said, "Paris can give me everything — except happiness." . . . . and so her childhood dream became a FORGOTTEN DREAM, and she remained the friend of the poor for the rest of her life!

SWEET DREAMS!

(Ian plays out with a further 25 seconds of "Forgotten Dreams")

FRIDAY

(Cue Ian at piano . . . . 30 seconds of "The Impossible Dream")

To dream the impossible dream, to fight the unbeatable foe, to reach the unreachable star . . . . to stretch oneself to achieve the seemingly unachievable — that's the song's philosophy, and it's not a bad one!

The world's greatest achievements started out as someone's "impossible dream" — history is full of them — people who dreamt dreams and who strived relentlessly to transform these dreams into reality — and who, despite the setbacks, refused point blank to throw in the towel!

As the words of another song reminds us, "Nothing's impossible" . . . .

"Think of the number of famous men
who had to fall and rise again, so
Pick yourself up, dust yourself down
And start all over again!"

One famous man in particular springs to mind who had to fall and rise again. "HE descended into hell," the ancient creed tells us, AND "He ascended into heaven." His name is of course Jesus Christ.

And as he assures us in the Bible, with God, there is NOTHING — no hope, no plan, no dream which is IMPOSSIBLE. With HIM all things are possible!

A very good and peaceful night, and of course, SWEET DREAMS!

(Ian plays out with a further 30 seconds of "The Impossible Dream")

12

"The times are a-changing"

I sent a postcard recently to a friend — a friend whom I thought might appreciate my rather peculiar sense of humour! Down in the corner of the front of the card was a line drawing of a certain well known writer who hailed from Stratford-upon-Avon, and the words above ran as follows: "SO I HAVEN'T WRITTEN MUCH RECENTLY — SO WHAT? NEITHER HAS SHAKESPEARE!" (The postcard was not sent to the editor of "The People's Friend" let me stress!)

But the venue from which the card was sent was none other than Stratford-upon-Avon. I had always wanted to visit the famous town, where in April 1564, the greatest name in the world of literature was born, and a few months ago I had the opportunity to do so while in the area, not only to see the famous town but to knock on the door of its most famous son. (He wasn't in!)

Shakespeare's house, Stratford-Upon-Avon.

However after spending some time in and around his birthplace I went on to visit the Royal Shakespeare Theatre and also the most marvellous audio-visual presentation entitled "The World Of Shakespeare" in which the audience travel back in time to the atmosphere of Elizabethan England. By using sophisticated technology, viewers are able to share in the sights and sounds and bustle and noise of everyday sixteenth century life.

What's more, they are able, in the company of the young William Shakespeare, to share in the dramatic events that were part and parcel of his childhood in that beautiful market town as it was in days of yore!

The times, of course, have changed almost beyond recognition and the sights and sounds of yesteryear, generally speaking, bear little resemblance to those of today, whether in Stratford-upon-Avon or in any other sixteenth century market town the length and breadth of the land.

People too have changed over the years — at least as far as their outward appearance is concerned they have changed! But inwardly aren't the folks of today much the same as the folks of yesterday? They share the same hopes and longings for themselves, for their families and for their dear ones, they share in their loved ones' fears and worries, in their joys and in their sorrows.

"The times are a-changing" as the popular folk song reminds us, but some things never change, and, it must be said, some people and their memory live on throughout the changing years — like the Bard of Stratford — William Shakespeare!

But there is another who lives on as year succeeds year, and whose love and whose assurance is available to each one of us day in, day out as we grapple with the things that concern us and our families while we try to live out our lives in a changing world.

His name is Jesus Christ — and he — as the Bible reminds us — is the same, yesterday, today and forever!

An undercover story!

NOW here's an undercover story if ever there was one! It all happened about ten years ago when I had just arrived in Nairn as the new parish minister — although the lady at the centre of the story only confessed all to me a few weeks ago! "I know you much better now Ian, so I think I can let you in on a wee secret concerning something that happened a long time ago." "Whatever is coming?" I thought to myself as I settled back to listen to Jean's revealing tale!

Not long after I had arrived in the town, Jean Cameron had taken ill and was admitted to the local County Hospital. While she was there as a patient, the hospital staff, on a particular day, were busy organising a rather special party. A fellow patient of Jean's — and much more senior in years let me emphasise! — was about to celebrate her 90th birthday. Jean, with the full agreement of the hospital staff of course, thought it would be a nice idea if they could all enjoy a wee glass of sherry to toast the birthday girl on her "big day". So she asked her son David to bring in to the hospital two bottles of sherry on the day before the party. This he duly did — but who do you think arrived hard on David's tail to visit his mother but the new parish minister — namely yours truly!

Propped up in bed, bottles in hand, Jean suddenly saw me coming down the ward! "Oh goodness, here's the minister — what on earth will I do?" In a flash she slipped the two bottles under her bedclothes just in time to greet the new minister with a smile — who of course hadn't noticed Jean's predicament! The minister sat down to have a wee chat with Jean — and where do you think he sat? Yes, as David was sitting on the bedside chair, yours truly apparently sat on Jean's bed!

As she revealed to me recently, "Ian, you'll never know how worried I was that these bottles would start to "clank" together under the bedclothes — I was a nervous wreck! And you'll never appreciate how glad I was to see my new minister leave!"

Jean is much better now, and the dear ninety-year-old, if she is still with us, must be nearing her century, but what a laugh we had when Jean revealed the secret she had been "bottling up" for all those years!

You know, in a much more serious vein, all of us have something we want to hide from other people. There are things each one of us do, and think and feel from time to time that we simply wouldn't wish to reveal, not even to those closest to us.

But of course although we can hide things from others — even from the minister! — there is nothing we can ever hide from our Maker. God knows the innermost secrets of our hearts and minds, indeed he knows each one of us even better than we know ourselves, because He is ALL knowing, ALL seeing, ALL loving and "nearer to us than breathing". The well loved children's hymn sums it up for us so perfectly:

"GOD IS ALWAYS NEAR ME, HEARING WHAT I SAY,
KNOWING ALL MY THOUGHTS AND DEEDS,
ALL MY WORK AND PLAY."

"Food for thought"

THE main function of the Moderator in the court which we call "Presbytery" in the Church of Scotland is to chair the monthly meetings.

Additionally however, the Moderator is often invited during his year of office to officiate at all kinds of services, events and functions in the various churches which are located within the Presbytery's area. Moderators for example, are often asked to open and dedicate new churches, or new church halls, or to dedicate newly renovated church premises. And although I was much involved in many alternative moderatorial pursuits, I must say that none of these particular duties came my way during my year as Moderator!

However, just towards the end of my "year" I WAS invited to open . . . . not a newly built or refurbished Church or Church hall, but a newly refurbished KITCHEN! And what's more it all took place in a house just a few doors along from our manse!

Our friends had just had new units etc. installed in their kitchen and in order to celebrate they thought that a party might be the order of the day. Better still, why not organise an official "opening" — and who better (they thought!) to say a few words and cut the red ribbon than the Moderator of the Presbytery — rather, their friend yours truly!

Needless to say the Moderator accepted their invitation and took it as a great compliment to be invited to preside on such an auspicious occasion. Not only did he take it as a compliment, he took the matter with great seriousness as he pondered on what he might say on the day. Obviously the occasion demanded a "seasoned" word, palatable, tasteful, and one which would give those present "food for thought"!

The great day arrived and there we all were huddled together in the lovely refurbished kitchen at No. 45. Just before I cut the red tape, which stretched from the breakfast bar over to the sink unit, and following a few rather predictable "wise cracks" from the officiating guest — which illicited the rather predictable response which friends tend to make! — I went on to assure those present at the kitchen cabinet meeting that what we were about had, in a very real kind of away, even biblical connotations.

Rather more seriously I took the opportunity to remind my friends that we read in the gospel of Martha preparing food for Jesus himself in the house where she lived with her sister at Bethany — and presumably she did so in the KITCHEN!

The kitchen is a symbol of home — indeed it has been described as the heart of the home. It's the place where people gather together. Perhaps you've heard the popular and anonymous "kitchen" rhyme which runs like this:

"No matter where I serve my guests,
it seems they like my kitchen best!"

Kitchens are places where families particularly gather together — it's there, around the table, that they eat together, talk together and share together . . . . reminiscent perhaps of another table at which Jesus once sat — although on that occasion, he SERVED.

And 2,000 years on, the family of Jesus in churches and in homes throughout the world still gather together around that table to share joyfully in his love and in his life!

The Communion Table in Nairn Old Parish Church.

"I can sing a rainbow"

F OLLOWING the success of "Joseph and the Technicolor Dreamcoat" and "Jonah-Man Jazz" in recent years, the boys and girls of Nairn Old Senior Sunday School took to the boards once again (at least, to the church chancel!) with this year's production, "Noah and the Ark".

The church was packed as usual for their performance which was presented to the congregation at the end of our annual Sunday School Prizegiving Service, and it must be said, the children rose to the occasion. To say the least — they were marvellous!

The Sunday School staff had obviously spent many a long hour preparing costumes and scenery for the production — not to mention the time they had taken to assist the children with the script and the songs, which, as ever came over word perfect!

In the context of the bible story, as many will remember, God had decided to destroy mankind because of all the violence and wickedness in the world he had created. Noah however, being an upright, kindly and honourable man — the only one left according to God! — would escape the wrath of the Almighty. He was given divine instructions to build a boat in which he and his wife, plus his three sons and their wives had to take refuge during the tempest-tossed days ahead. In addition to his nearest and dearest, Noah was told to take with him into his Ark numerous varieties of birds and animals — two of each, male and female.

Now let me say at once that the Parish Kirk in Nairn WASN'T transformed into an ecclesiastical zoo for the production! Rather, the boys and girls were dressed as various animals, and hand in hand they boarded the large boat that Noah (with a little bit of help from the Sunday School teachers!) had painstakingly contructed for the performance!

The duration of the original old testament story spanned many many days and months. The bible tells us that when the flood came, it continued for forty days, the water didn't start to subside for a further one hundred and fifty days, and only on the 17th day of the 7th month did the Ark come to rest on the top of Mount Ararat. However the Nairn Old production didn't take quite as long — in fact it was all squeezed in to a little more than 25 minutes!

Nevertheless, the message of the story portrayed by the boys and girls came through loud and clear, especially as they joined in the song, "I can sing a rainbow".

The rainbow at the end of the story of Noah, as the children so cogently reminded us, was God's sign that he would never again destroy the earth, either by a flood or by any other means. God's very words were these: "Whenever the rainbow appears in the clouds I will see it and remember my everlasting covenant between me and all living beings."

The words of the children's final song put it this way — "WHENEVER YOU SEE A RAINBOW, REMEMBER GOD IS LOVE!"

The boys' and girls' performance was every bit as colourful as a rainbow, let me assure you — and its memory will be lasting . . . . as is the love of God of which the rainbow so vividly speaks!

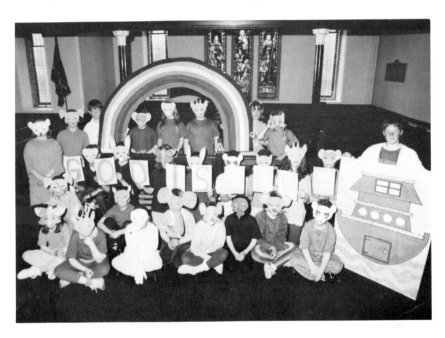

A Right Royal Occasion!

DURING a recent visit to London, Margaret and I had the opportunity to visit the famous Royal Opera House in Covent Garden — and to sit in the Royal Box! Let me explain.

We hadn't realised it before arriving in the capital city, but over that particular weekend, access to and conducted tours of notable buildings not normally open to the public, were being given, free of charge, as part of the "Open House" programme, which was operating simultaneously throughout Europe. In fact we managed to see through quite a few famous London landmarks during our short time there, including The Law Courts, Ealing Studios, the B.B.C., and of course, The Royal Opera House.

The Royal Opera House, Covent Garden.

First of all we were led through the grandeur of the main foyer into the Victorian Auditorium which seats 2,156 people! The beauty and splendour of its domed ceiling and decor is sumptuous, to say the least. Our lady guide told us that it is the only surviving horse-shoe shaped theatre in London without overhanging balconies, and the famous Proscenium Arch above the huge stage, which depicts poetry and music, with the bust of Queen Victoria in central position, is absolutely breathtaking!

"Would you care to go up now to the Royal Box?" our guide kindly enquired. "Just try and stop us!" I was tempted to respond! En route to the Royal Box we were ushered through the "King's Smoking Room" which was regularly used by Edward 7th, and it is said that the room is a replica of his cabin on the former Royal Yacht, "Victoria and Albert". From there we climbed up aloft to the Ante Room of the Royal Box, where, we were told, the Royal Family often dine prior to performances. "Can I now invite you to take your seats in the Royal Box?" our guide amusingly suggested!

In the box are two large and beautifully padded chairs (almost like thrones!) which came it is thought from the Great Exhibition of 1851, and needless to say, yours truly — and his queen! — had a wee seat on them for a few happy and glorious minutes . . . . and what a view of the stage and auditorium!

Queen Victoria it seems was a regular visitor to the Royal Opera House, as are several members of the present Royal Family, but Victoria once ordered that a mirror be hung on one of the walls of the Royal Box, and she had it so positioned that her ladies-in-waiting could see the performance from their places on the sofa behind! What a kindly, thoughtful gesture!

It was a memorable visit, and what a privilege it was to sit there on these "royal thrones" albeit for a few brief and magical moments!

As we made our way back down to earth from these regal dizzy heights the whole experience brought very cogently to mind a not dissimilar kind of occasion recorded in new testament times when the King of Kings lived among us, an occasion when two of Jesus' closest friends, James and John, had asked in effect for seats in the Royal Box! They had heard Jesus talking about the coming of his Kingdom and I suppose they imagined that they should have key positions within it. If Jesus was to be King, they being among his closest and most faithful friends, should at least have high-ranking positions in his court. And so they petitioned Jesus, "Master when you sit on your throne in your glorious Kingdom, we want you to let us sit with you, one at your right, and one at your left."

Of course they had got it all wrong — they were looking for a short cut to glory! Jesus however soon put them right by explaining to them that the only way to his kind of glory was via a life of service, suffering and sacrifice, the kind of life Jesus himself had led.

That's the way it is for all who seek to follow and serve this King . . . . and as Jesus further explained to his misguided friends James and John . . . . as for the seats in the Royal Box? GOD WILL ALLOCATE THESE TO THOSE FOR WHOM HE HAS PREPARED THEM.

GRAMPIAN TELEVISION

SOME MORE "REFLECTIONS" . . . .

MONDAY

(Cue Ian at piano . . . . 20 seconds of "You need hands")

Nice to be with you again . . . . and maybe you recognised that song . . . . "YOU NEED HANDS" . . . . and you DO need hands to play a piano!

You know, people often say to me following "Reflections" . . . . "Whenever I see those hands on the keyboard, I know it's you!"

I don't suppose many folks are recognised by their hands — yet I don't know — hands are quite revealing. They tell you a lot about a person.

Fingerprints are a most positive means of identification . . . . and then there's the strength of a handshake. The way in which some of us gesticulate expresses our personality so they say. Hands reveal many occupations . . . . the white, rather softer hands of the office worker . . . . the grime-ingrained hands of the mechanic or engineer . . . . the calloused hands of a tradesman.

Have you ever tried to picture the hands of Jesus? They would be pretty rough and calloused too I imagine — he was a tradesman.

But do you remember, after Jesus rose from the dead, Thomas in search of proof asked to inspect Jesus' hands. The picture he saw is almost too painful to contemplate.

The once-calloused carpenter's hands were now suffering, nail-pierced hands — proclaiming that God's love is so great that he is willing to live and die for all his people. Jesus' hands assure EVERYONE who suffers that God is present with them in their suffering.

"You need hands to thank the Lord for living" the song concludes . . . . yes, that's true . . . . but you need hands also to thank the Lord for DYING.

A very good and peaceful night.

(No music at end of programme — out on G.T.V. caption)

TUESDAY

(Cue Ian at piano . . . . 25 seconds of "I want to hold your hand")

"I want to hold your hand" — a Lennon and McCartney classic. And there's a lot of merit in the concept . . . . holding each other's hand!

"An' there's a hand my trusty fiere, an' gei's a hand o' thine" wrote our national bard. A firm, welcoming handshake establishes an immediate warm contact one to another. But so often in life people are just crying out for someone to hold their hand.

In situations of illness — anxiety — hopelessness and of bereavement. Especially in times of sorrow folks often just need someone to hold their hand . . . . either physically or metaphorically . . . . just to BE THERE to support and help them through their time of loss.

How often we read in the New Testament of Jesus holding the hand of another or taking someone by the hand. THAT is what many of the clamouring crowds that followed Jesus wanted . . . . to know the touch of the Master's hand.

"Jesus, I want to hold your hand!" cried out the blind, the leper and the lame. And to each of these the touch of Jesus brought life and health and strength and sight, because Jesus' hands were HEALING hands, and today he uses OUR hands to help bring his healing to one another.

(Ian plays out with a further 30 seconds of the song "I want to hold your hand")

WEDNESDAY

(Cue Ian at piano . . . . 20 seconds of "Jesus' hands were kind hands")

No — don't go reaching for your French dictionaries — it's a traditional French tune I know, but it's set in the Church Hymn Book to the words; "Jesus' hands were kind hands doing good to all."

And it's so TRUE, day in, day out Jesus used his hands in the service of others . . . . and for any one of us to do the same is undoubtedly CHRISTLIKE.

I read recently a story, an old but true story of a girl in her early twenties who lay very ill in hospital. She was in the final stages of T.B. The eldest in a poor and large family, her mother had died at the birth of the youngest child, and for years the girl had "spent herself" looking after the home and "mothering" the younger children. Her face was drawn, her hands were rough, weak, worn and workstained.

A church worker came to visit her — a rather, let's say, "enthusiastic" church worker, who began to pound the poor girl with question after question! Had she gone to Sunday School? Had she been baptised? Had she been confirmed? Had she gone to church regularly?

To all these questions the dying girl gave a weary "No". But what will you do when you die and have to tell God all that?

She said very softly and simply: "I WILL SHOW HIM MY HANDS." Goodnight.

(Ian plays out with a further 20 seconds of "Jesus' hands were kind hands")

THURSDAY

(Cue Ian at piano . . . . 25 seconds of "Put your hand in the hand of the Man from Galilee")

"Put your hand in the hand of the Man from Galilee" . . . . now that's good thinking . . . . hand in hand with God! Because you see that's how God gets things done in the world — it's a working partnership . . . . and in a sense, God is just as helpless without US as we are without HIM!

For example, if God wants a sick person cured, he has to get a physician to bring to that person his healing power. The Almighty needs his fellow-labourers!

A well known minister used to tell this story . . . . about a man who had an allotment, and when he got it, it was waste ground — full of weeds, wild grass, stones and rocks. But after HARD TOIL he was able to grow the most luscious vegetables and the most beautiful flowers.

When showing his allotment to a rather pious friend, the friend remarked, "Isn't it wonderful what God can do and make grow on a bit of ground?" "Yes" said the man, "but you should have seen it when God had it to himself!"

The veg and flowers could never have been grown without the sweat and toil of God's partner working hand in hand with him. And that's true in every area. Someone once put it this way:

"He has no hands but our hands to do his work today,
He has no feet but our feet to lead folks in his way,
He has no voice but our voice to tell folks how he died,
He has no help but our help to lead folks to his side."

Join hands with God . . . . enter into a divine, co-operating partnership . . . . and put YOUR hand in the hand of the Man from Galilee! Goodnight.

(Ian plays out with 25 seconds of "Put your hand in the hand of the Man from Galilee")

FRIDAY

(Cue Ian at piano . . . . 30 seconds of "He's got the whole world in his hands")

"He's got the whole world in his hands" — that's a real showstopper! . . . . but HAS he? HAS God got the whole world in his hands?

When you look out on the world scene — the trouble spots — the disaster areas — poverty — hunger — war . . . . and suffering at home, maybe even on your own doorstep . . . . and so MUCH of that suffering we believe to be undeserved.

"What have I done to deserve this?" — the age-old question. If God has all the power — and if God loves us — if he HAS the whole world in his hands, then why oh why does he permit all this?

24

Pain and suffering IS a mystery and there's no simple solution. The innocent DO perish and sometimes the most godly people have to carry the heaviest of burdens. We simply don't HAVE all the answers.

But remember this — GOD was no stranger to suffering. In Jesus Christ — and especially in his crucifixion — God suffered agony in the extreme . . . . and in consequence, HE is right there with US, be sure.

The story is told of a very upset child. Dad came into his bedroom to comfort him. He lay down beside his son and listened . . . . and after the young boy had cried his problem out, Dad eased his way out of the bed and out of the room. In changing his position for sleep the boy moved over to where his FATHER had been lying . . . . and he found that DAD'S pillow was wet also. His father had been crying with him — AS OUR HEAVENLY FATHER MOST SURELY CRIES WITH US.

Have a good and peaceful night in the assurance that God HAS the whole world in his caring, LOVING hands.

(Ian plays out with a further 30 seconds of "He's got the whole world in his hands")

Eden, a Garden of Remembrance

DURING a recent holiday in Yorkshire we went along to visit Eden Camp, just outside Malton. Originally it was Prisoner of War Camp No. 83 which housed initially Italian P.O.W's. and later on during the war years, many German servicemen.

The old camp has been most imaginatively made into a modern history museum — the only type in the world — and, I must say, it well deserves the many awards and commendations it has won.

It seemed particularly significant during this year when as a nation we have commemorated V.E.Day and V.J. Day to be transported back to Wartime Britain. Each P.O.W. hut there is in effect a chapter in the story of the Second World War. But Eden Camp is more than that, it is a living experience of what it was like to live from day to day during these terrible war years both at home and on the battle front.

By using sound and lighting, smoke generators and even smells, visitors are made to feel that they are actually there in the particular wartime situation! In one hut you are able to experience what it is like in a submarine under attack by a German U-boat, in another you can experience a British town under seige during the terrible blitz, and in yet another you can take a trip down a coalmine in the company of the Bevin Boys.

The children were intrigued to learn about things like clothing coupons, "Make do and mend", the Land Army, and not least rationing. As a post-war baby (just!) I can well remember accompanying my mother to the local grocer in Glasgow with her Ration Book in hand! Perhaps many "Friend" readers will remember precisely these wartime rations: During 1940 each person was allowed 12ozs. of sugar per week, 4ozs. of butter and approximately 1 lb. of meat. Tea, margarine and cooking fat were rationed at 2 ozs. per week. Sugar for cake icing was prohibited and tiered wedding cakes were often made of cardboard and hired from the baker! In 1941 the cheese ration had been cut to 1 oz. per person per week and the following year people were asked not to exceed five inches of water in their bath in order to save fuel! We just don't know we're living today!

It was a wonderful experience altogether, yet it was also very moving for a later generation to witness there at first hand the hardships, grief, suffering and sacrifice both at home and abroad during these terrible war years.

The Chapel, Eden Camp

Towards the end of the exhibition visitors move on to one of its newest features. One of the huts that used to house the wartime prisoners has been made into the most beautiful Chapel, and on the interior walls of this place of peace several memorial plaques have already been installed.

But for me, the most moving aspect of all was the Altar Cross which depicts Jesus hanging on it. It's story was remarkable — it had been beautifully and painstakingly carved — out of a Red Cross Box! — by a wartime prisoner. Here we saw grief, suffering and sacrifice at its utmost.

As we made our way back to the car, we passed the Camp's most poignant War Memorial standing between the huts, the barbed wire fencing and the watchtowers. It too had a cross on it, with these words: "Eden Camp Modern History Museum was created to honour the courage, fortitude and sacrifice of the people who served in all walks of life during the Second World War, 1939-1945".

At this time of year — and especially perhaps this 50th Anniversary Year — we remember of course with pride and with thanksgiving those who fell in two world wars and in other wars since. But as the memorial at Eden Camp so cogently reminds us, we must remember those who served in all walks of life then that we may live in peace now.

The War Memorial and Watchtower, Eden Camp

27

A Trilogy of Christmas Thoughts
i) "ONLY MAKE BELIEVE?"

A few weeks ago I had the privilege and pleasure of providing the piano accompaniments for a singer friend of mine who was performing in the area. She really is blessed with the most wonderful singing voice, and as a semi-professional her repertoire is extensive to say the least — from Bach to Beatles, classics to pop, sacred to secular — with a dash of "Scottish" thrown in for good measure!

My friend is particularly fond of many of the songs from the musicals that have been produced over the years and on this recent occasion she included in her varied programme the legendary Jerome Kern song "Make Believe" from his hit-musical, "Showboat".

The sentiments which the song's title suggest are not in fact all that inappropriate at this time of year as we approach Christmas. Right now we're at the peak of a kind of "transformation scene". Suddenly and amazingly, albeit temporarily our world has been transformed into a kind of fairyland, make-believe world in which "sleighbells ring, snowflakes glisten" (even if it's only the artificial variety!) and lights twinkle!

CHRISTMAS and CHILDREN seem to go hand in hand, and in truth I suppose this has always been so! Santa's visit to THEIR house is uppermost in their minds at this time, and by courtesy of "Santa," very shortly there will be children throughout the world opening parcels and emptying stockings which have been painstakingly wrapped and lovingly filled full and running over!

While we associate this happy event especially with the young ones, and while we must admit that these few short weeks of magic and make-believe are unarguably directed towards their generation — by no means is it KID'S STUFF. Certainly we rejoice with them on Christmas morning when we see their faces light up as all their dreams come true, but by no means is the occasion for them exclusively.

The event, which all began with a child remember, is for all God's created children everywhere — of all ages! Christmas is nothing less than the incarnation, the birth of the Saviour of the World . . . . "WHICH SHALL BE FOR ALL PEOPLE" as the lovely gospel story reminds us. Stripping the event of all its magical and make-believe trappings — necessary as all of these are let it be said — Christmas is the most cogent reminder to one and to all that giving started for real when God gave his only Son, Jesus, to the children of men.

But back to the song . . . . "We could make-believe I love you, only make-believe that you love me", to quote Oscar Hammerstein's opening lyrics. Ah, but it's at this point, when we turn to the words, that the inappropriateness of the song begins to become evident. Because you see, when it comes to God's love for us and our love for him, anything "make-believe" is simply not on!

His love for us is real, it's lasting . . . . and it's forever! There's certainly nothing make-believe about the love that came down at the first Christmas in the form of the child in the manger at Bethlehem!

And for us to offer in return ANYTHING LESS . . . . would be childish. HAPPY CHRISTMAS!

ii) CHRISTMAS . . . . STICK AT IT!

IN recent years I have had the great privilege of participating in summer pulpit exchanges to New Jersey. While there last July a friend presented me with a book in which I read the rather amusing story of an American minister — a bit of a D.I.Y. enthusiast — who had received, on the previous Christmas morning, the gift of an electric glue-gun!

Now to say that yours truly is a bit of a D.I.Y. enthusiast would be stretching the truth to a quite ridiculous extent! Nevertheless, as this stylish, sensational, superlative electric glue-gun was described in the story — as only the Americans know how — I must confess, I did contemplate the many uses to which such a product might be put by a member of the clergy!

Indeed a very practical purpose comes to mind immediately. The slippers I am wearing as I write this Christmas article — one of them has a rather floppy sole . . . . and as ministers must always display concern for floppy soles (or is it sloppy souls!) perhaps such a product might come in useful here! Of course, maybe if I hold off until Christmas morning the situation will be remedied when I unwrap my presents . . . . if it's not too late to drop hints in the direction of my family!

However as I read on and contemplated my American counterpart's newfangled toy I imagined all sorts of practical, pastoral situations in which I might be able to use an electric glue-gun if one came my way. For example the kind of situation in which a family were at war with each other, broken in unity, through animosity, arguments, bitterness and ill-feeling. Then along comes the family minister for a counselling session with them. In my imagination I could hear myself saying to the feuding family; "Now all join hands and let's have a prayer together," and then when everyone's eyes were closed I would reach for my electric glue-gun and zap them with it just as their hands joined — and say further, "Right, go and work things out together" Never would that family have been so together in a long time!

Weddings — now there's another pastoral situation in which I could use my new toy. "Will you give each other the right hand?" the Minister says — followed by a quick shot of glue from the gun — and the next phrase, "this man and woman joined together" would take on an entirely new

30

meaning! "To have and to hold from this day forward" would most certainly be for real!

Or again at the point in the Service of Admission when newly admitted members shake hands with the Minister and elders — "joining the church" would be seen in a new light, and if those concerned were ever asked if they had a church connection, they could answer hand on heart that they sure had!

But as I would continue to contemplate my new toy rather more seriously I would very soon conclude that NO super glue-gun would ever solve the broken situations of life that touch and affect each one of us sooner or later.

BROKEN DREAMS perhaps . . . . things just haven't worked out as you thought they would . . . . the job hasn't gone as you imagined it would . . . . or maybe the job has gone full stop. Or BROKEN RELATIONSHIPS . . . . there are so many of these, within the family, within the community, among the neighbours or within the Church. And reconciliation is never easy. Or it may be a BROKEN MARRIAGE. "What God has joined together" man has, and man IS, more and more, putting asunder.

Perhaps your life is broken by PAIN and SUFFERING, or perhaps it's your HEART that's been broken by bereavement and by loss. Bereavement is a storm . . . . and it's a terrifying, shattering one. Riding it out is never easy. Indeed there are so many other situations of brokenness that afflict and beset us all. And in truth it takes a lot more than my American friend's super glue-gun to cope with all of these!

Goodwill toward Men

God has been described as "the one in whom all things hold together." You see, the mystery and wonder of Christmas is simply this, namely that in the birth of the Christchild, the one who holds all things together visited our world — in the words of the lovely carol, "He came down to earth from heaven, who is GOD and Lord of all!" And He alone is the source of healing for all the brokenness we experience. EVERYTHING ELSE HAS FAILED! I'm reminded also of the great Advent Hymn which runs like this: "He comes, the broken hearts to bind, the bleeding souls to cure, and with the treasures of his grace, to enrich the humble poor."

THIS is what the lovely gospel stories of shepherds, wise men, angels, the manger, the gold and frankincense and myrrh are REALLY all about! This is what CHRISTMAS is all about — it's about God breaking in in a most unique way, once and FOR ALL, to mend the brokenness of his creation!

The Christchild, who came at Christmas and who later began his work by mending ploughs went on to mend men and women broken in mind, body and spirit, and he concluded his work by mending the world!

If you will make room for Him in your life, in your family and in your heart this Christmas, be sure, He can and will mend you too — whatever the nature of your brokenness! He can restore you and He can make you whole. "There is a balm in Gilead to make the wounded whole" — and never are we more cogently reminded of this than at Christmas when we see IN THE FLESH the God in whom all things are held together!

May His peace and joy be experienced among you and your loved ones this Christmastide.

iii) CHRISTMAS . . . . A FAMILY AFFAIR

As a minister of the gospel I am very much encouraged to see that for many families, the Church still has an important role to play within their lives. Many people bring their babies to church for baptism — many young couples still seek a church wedding — and most families still turn to the church for comfort in a time of bereavement and loss. In addition of course, countless families support the church Sunday by Sunday by attending church services, and in so many other ways. It's worth noting that in Scotland, more folk attend church worship on a Sunday than attend football matches on a Saturday! So it's good to know (especially during this year which marks the "International Year of the Family") that for so many families throughout the world, the church is still seen to have an important place in their lives.

As Christmas rapidly approaches we are reminded that this time in the year is particularly associated with family get-togethers! It's sometimes difficult to believe that "Christmas comes but once a year" because it seems only weeks since I was busy getting Christmas material gathered together and Christmas services prepared, but in fact one full calendar year has almost elapsed! How time flies!

Christmas on the one hand, and children on the other would in these days seem synonymous. Yet I suppose this has been the case throughout the ages! "It's really for the children, isn't it?" is the rather typical seasonal cliché that we hear. Certainly Santa Claus still tops the popularity polls at this time of year for so many young folks, and throughout the length and breadth of the world around now boys and girls will be starting to put down on paper their Christmas list for "Santa" in the hope that he will fill their stockings and pillowcases to the brim with all sorts of good and lovely things!

Santa Claus, or St. Nicholas as he was originally and more properly known, was in fact a bishop in the Christian Church some 1600 years ago at a place called Myra in Asia Minor. Adopted as the patron saint of Russia and of sailors — as well as of children! — it's said that he traditionally brought gifts on his feast day which was December 6th.

Additionally another story surrounds him that would seem to add weight to the "Santa" legend which has been handed down. In the town where St. Nicholas lived, there lived also a very poor family — a man and his three daughters, none of whom could marry because they didn't have the money for a dowry. However St. Nicholas came to the rescue by quietly and stealthily visiting the house in the dead of night and by dropping a bag of gold through the WINDOW — who knows where the chimney myth came from!

Now the first daughter, the eldest, could marry — and subsequently, so the story goes, he did the same for the other two daughters — and all lived happily ever after! No doubt this Christmas, St. Nicholas or "Santa" will bring similar joy to children in families everywhere as he has done throughout the centuries — let's hope so!

However let us all realise that, despite the popular seasonal cliché, Christmas isn't just for the children — at least, not just for them alone. While we delight as we see their faces beam with joy during this happy time ahead, let us be ever conscious that the event, the incarnation of the Saviour of the World, is for God's children of all ages and in all places. Christmas is a family affair — it's for the families of the world!

At this season of gaiety and gladness we remember that the giving of Christmas gifts started for real, not with St. Nicholas or "Santa" but with a family in Bethlehem — a very special family we often refer to as The Holy Family. God's unique gift came in the form of his only Son, the Manger Child who was given to the Family of Man as a Saviour. "You shall give him the name Jesus (Saviour)" said the angel, "For he will save his people from their sins."

The official year which has marked the "International Year of the Family" will shortly draw to a close, but let each one of us remember that every year in history can be, for every nation throughout the world, the Year of the Family, thanks to the priceless gift of the Father of all families.

And as we look forward, after the event, to a new year ahead, let us remember that our hopes for the future — and indeed the hope for the future of the world in our time — is to be found alone in the heart of this little child of the Holy Family.

> "Then a shoot shall grow from the stock of Jesse . . . . the spirit of the Lord shall rest upon him, a spirit of wisdom, understanding, counsel and power. He shall judge the poor with justice and defend the humble with equity. Then the wolf shall live with the sheep, and the leopard lie down with the kid. The calf and the young lion shall grow up together . . . . AND A LITTLE CHILD SHALL LEAD THEM." (ISAIAH Chapter 11)

MAY THE PEACE, JOY AND LOVE WHICH THE LITTLE CHILD BRINGS WITH HIM BLESS YOU AND YOUR FAMILIES AT CHRISTMAS AND THROUGHOUT THE COMING YEAR.

GRAMPIAN TELEVISION

SOME NEW YEAR "REFLECTIONS"

MONDAY

(Cue Ian at piano . . . . 30 seconds of "Those were the days")

Hello again, and on this second day of the new year A VERY HAPPY NEW YEAR to you and yours! "Those were the days my friend, I thought they'd never end, we'd sing and dance for ever and a day" . . . . maybe you're STILL singing and dancing to welcome in 1995 . . . . but whether you are or not, DAYS are going to be this week's theme.

"THOSE were the days" . . . . how often we hear that said — or — "The Good Old Days" . . . . that used to be a T.V. programme too! Many like to claim that this age is unique, that never before have people had to cope with so many difficulties and complexities in terms of living out their lives. If you examine history in fact I think you'll find that EVERY age has brought in its train its own peculiar problems!

Nevertheless, "Those were the days!" The Children of Israel said it away back in Old Testament history when they were wandering, apparently hopelessly, in the desert. "You should have left us in Egypt" they complained to Moses . . . . "we had food and water and shelter there!' But were THEIR "old" days really so good? . . . . They were slaves remember.

In truth, for us all, in terms of days gone by, some WERE good . . . . and some not so good perhaps — that's the mixture-maxture life metes out!

Try THIS as a formula for living out YOUR days: Live with thanks for the days that were — live with joyful expectation for the days that are — and live with faith in God for the days and years that are yet to be! . . . . Enjoy the rest of TODAY and I'll see you again tomorrow"

(Ian plays out with a further 20 seconds of "Those were the days")

TUESDAY

(Cue Ian at piano . . . . 25 seconds of "Day by Day")

Do you remember that lively number from the musical "Godspell"? "Day by day, day by day, O dear Lord, three things I PRAY". It's a song about prayer . . . . "to see you more clearly, to love you more dearly, to follow you more nearly" . . . . and the song ends rather repetitively — certainly as far as the lyrics are concerned it is repetitive — no less than four "Day by days"

36

one after the other! "Day by day, by day by day, by day by day, by day by day . . . ." I think that was four!

But do you see the point the song is making? Prayer must be repetitive . . . . repetitive in the REGULAR sense . . . . not just when we're up against it or when we're in trouble (although God listens to our prayers then to be sure!) But for the writer of the song, prayer must be a regular habit — as indeed it was for Jesus.

Often we read in the gospel of Jesus taking time out for regular prayer, in order that HE could see God HIS Father more clearly, love HIM more dearly and follow HIM more nearly. And if PRAYER was a necessity for Jesus Christ, how much more necessary must it be for you and me? . . . . Not just occasionally . . . . not even just on Sundays . . . . but DAY BY DAY BY DAY BY DAY . . . . and I hope you're having a good one!

(Ian plays out with a further 25 seconds of "Day by day")

WEDNESDAY

(Cue Ian at piano . . . . 30 seconds of "What a difference a day makes")

Hello again. That song 'had its day' quite a number of years ago . . . . but it's still popular — "What a difference a day makes", And the sentiments the song expresses are still popular too, because it's true, the passage of a day can literally turn your life upside down!

This happens because the day has perhaps brought sad circumstances into your life and that of your family . . . . or sometimes it's due to a happy event! Like the day on which our twin daughters were born — over fourteen years ago now — but life for us was never the same again after 1st February 1982!

What a difference a day makes! And that difference can be due to a letter, a phone call, a chance meeting . . . . whatever.

And when you turn to the Bible, and especially to the New Testament, you can read there of people whose lives were similarly turned upside down on the day they encountered a man called Jesus! Life for them thereafter was never the same!

People who had been lame found that they could walk again, many who suffered from blindness found they could see, deaf folks could hear and poor souls suffering from diseases of every ilk found themselves cured . . . . all due to an 'encounter of the day' with a man in whom they found the power to make them whole . . . . AND by displaying THEIR FAITH in the power this man undoubtedly possessed.

And then of course, there was a day later on in this man's life . . . . after he had been cruelly tortured, crucified and buried . . . . a SUNDAY . . . . and the difference THAT day made to the history of the world, was absolutely sensational! I do hope you're enjoying your day!

(Ian plays out with a further 20 seconds of "What a difference a day makes")

THURSDAY

(Cue Ian at piano . . . . 25 seconds of "One day at a time")

I hardly need to TELL you the name of that song . . . . but the sentiments it expresses are certainly very real, very dear to countless folks.

"One day at a time sweet Jesus,
that's all I'm asking from you —
Just give me the strength to do
every day what I have to do."

The lyrics of the song go on to mention the "stairways we each have to climb". How true . . . . life has often been compared to a steep stairway — or to an obstacle course . . . . and for so many, the stairway seems to get steeper and steeper, and the obstacles seem to appear with remarkable frequency . . . . just one after the other!

But take heart! Take one day at a time! At the START of each new day, with all the problems and perplexities, it MAY bring, ask God to help you handle the demands of the day AS IT COMES, and you'll find that the stairways, steep though they be, will be surmountable nevertheless in the presence of the One who gives us every new day . . . . AND who has promised to help us through each one of them! And have a very good and peaceful night.

(Ian plays out with a further 20 seconds of "One day at a time")

FRIDAY

(Cue Ian at piano . . . . 30 seconds of "May each day")

"May each day in the week be a good day" . . . . a song made popular some time ago by Andy Williams.

I do hope that YOU had some good days during the first week of this new year, and that these days will be repeated again and again as the days turn to months.

It was Oscar Wilde who said: "Each day is like a year, a year whose days are long". Well, I do hope that YOU won't find the days ahead too long, but whatever they may bring you, may I, on this final day of my "Reflections" meantime, leave you with these words from tonight's song as my prayer for you and yours. (IAN LIFTS SHEET MUSIC OF "MAY EACH DAY" FROM PIANO AND BRINGS INTO SHOT . . . . AND READS:) "May each day in the week be a good day — may the Lord always watch over you — and may all of your hopes turn to wishes — and may all of your wishes come true."

And may each one of you looking in be blessed day and daily by the One who is the same, "yesterday, today and forever!" . . . . AND, "Goodnight!"

(Ian plays a further 30 seconds of "May each day")

Majesty with Meekness

ON a recent visit to London, Margaret, the children and myself went along to Buckingham Palace to see the Royal Mews. After paying for our tickets we made our way out into the quadrangle around which the Mews are built. The first thing we noticed were two playful kittens jostling with one another on the ground — "No, these are NOT the Royal Mews!" I hastened to assure the Hamiltons!

In fact the word "mews" is an interesting one, and in origin it has nothing at all to do with stables, horses or carriages whatsoever! It comes from an old French word "mue" which means, "a changing — especially of a coat of feathers or skin." In the Middle Ages a "mews" was a place where a king's falcons were kept during their "mewing" period, or the time when their plumage changed.

So the King's Mews were originally "for the birds" — a place where his falcons were housed! But in 1537 the royal stables at Bloomsbury were razed to the ground by fire and the king at the time, Henry VIII, removed his falcons from their mews at Charing Cross to another venue, and he had his horses housed in what was the falcons' mews. Ever since, "mews" have been associated with horses, stables and carriages. So much for the history lesson!

As it happened, the day on which we visited the Royal Mews was bright and sunny, so all the carriages were wheeled out into the courtyard to give us a bird's eye view (oh no, we're back to these falcons again!) All the Queen's carriages, coaches and landaus were on display — including the Irish State Coach, the Scottish State Coach, the Australian State Coach, the Glass Coach (which has been used for almost all the royal weddings to transport the bride and groom back from the church to the palace) and not least THE State Coach — or the Golden Coach used by the monarch on the occasion of his or her Coronation — what a sight!

I was particularly interested in the Scottish State Coach. It's said that it is quite unique because the lower half of its body originally formed part of a glass coach built in the 1800's and in 1969 a totally new top section was constructed for it by St. Cuthbert's Co-operative Society in Edinburgh. It's also unique in that its roof is almost completely transparent which means that not only does it have extra light, but also, when the coach is out in procession, people above are able to look right down into it giving them a bird's eye view too! I was particularly interested to see the Royal Arms of Scotland and the insignia of the Order of the Thistle emblazoned on the side and doors of the Scottish Coach instead of the Royal Arms of England and the Order of the

The Scottish State Coach

Garter insignia borne by most of the others. Indeed it's said that of all the Queen's coaches, the Scottish State Coach is the lightest, brightest and most elegant — I would have to agree!

It's quite a sight to see the royal coaches out on parade, especially on occasions like coronations (I can just remember it!) or royal weddings, or when the the Queen makes an official royal visit to a particular town or country. Most of us I think delight in a sense of occasion and enjoy a bit of pomp and pageantry from time to time. Of course whenever and wherever the Queen goes in her official capacity as monarch, pomp, pageantry, flag-waving, cheering and ceremony are usually the keywords for these occasions . . . . a bit like the time, nearly 2,000 years ago when Jesus, the greatest King of all time, rode into Jerusalem in a kind of procession.

The bible tells us that there was waving and cheering as he made his royal way into the city — certainly there were no flags to wave in these days, but the peasant pilgrims who accompanied this king were excited by the crowds who lined the route and who waved palm branches they had cut down from the trees along the way! "Hosanna!" they shouted at the tops of their voices to greet THEIR King!

However on this occasion there were no carriages, no pomp, and no pageantry in the sense that we recognise it. Instead this king came riding on the back of a lowly donkey. "HUMILITY" was the keyword for this occasion — a KING of KINGS whose majesty was in his meekness — a King who rode to his royal throne on the back of a donkey.

"Hosanna to the King of Kings!"

All Thanks to a Stone!

THE response which I get from readers to "Manse Window" articles never ceases to amaze me — from all over the world! — and most of it is complimentary and encouraging let me assure you! But the response to a recent story was quite remarkable to say the least.

I had been telling "Friend" readers of the rather strange request I had received from the St. Andrew's Society of Winnipeg for a stone from the parish of Nairn. In fact they requested a stone from every parish in Scotland, each one to be inserted into a commemorative cairn which the Society were planning to build and to dedicate to all the Scots who had gone over to Canada, and especially Lord Thomas Selkirk, in the bitter days of the Highland Clearances during the early 1800's. The Nairn stone — from our lovely town's west beach — was duly despatched!

The Scots Monument, Winnipeg.

Following publication of the stone's story in the "Friend" I received a most charming and friendly letter from Mrs Jean McNicol of Alexandria

41

who had visited the monument just a few weeks before she read the "Manse Window" story! It has been in place for quite a while and it is situated on the banks of the Red River she tells me. The Scottish "parish" stones are incorporated into a semi-circular wall, with the monument, in the form of a thistle, right in the middle. On two of the sides of this monument there are plaques on which is engraved the names of all the parishes in Scotland which participated in the project. I must go over some day and look for "Nairn" — AND for the stone in the semi-circular wall, if I can find it!

In fact Jean's son is a member of the St.Andrew's Society of Winnipeg and he was present when the monument was recently dedicated by the Chaplain to the Society, the Rev. Donald Wilson. (Jean also kindly enclosed a photograph of the monument which is reproduced above.)

But — stone me — there's more! ANOTHER letter arrived at the manse two days later, also, and totally co-incidentally from the town of Alexandria, beside Loch Lomond! Rita Cameron wrote to say how much she had enjoyed the same "Manse Window" story and also to say how much she and her husband had enjoyed a short holiday in Nairn earlier in the year. During their holiday they spent a lot of time walking along our lovely beach here — collecting stones!

Rita and her friend Betty Bruce have the responsibility and the privilege of decorating their church in Jamestown for the Harvest Festival each year, and in her lovely letter she told me that this year they had decided to make the theme of one of their decorations, "The Harvest of the Sea". Rita's three-year-old grandson Christopher had helped her gather some more stones, this time from the "bonnie bonnie banks of Loch Lomond" on their doorstep. And yes, you've guessed, the stones from Nairn beach and those from Loch Lomond together helped grace the "Harvest of the Sea" display in church!

Harvest of course is all about SHARING, sharing the resources we have with other people who are less fortunate, and with other countries where the harvests have failed. But it was nice to learn that in a roundabout kind of a way, Nairn had a share in the Harvest Festival down there on Loch Lomondside — as well as in that rather unique harvest over there in Winnipeg! All thanks to a STONE — not altogether irrelevant in terms of the Christian faith. After all, it was all thanks to a stone, one which rolled away from the mouth of a borrowed tomb many centuries ago, that Christian people, from the shores of the Red River in Canada to the banks of Loch Lomond here in Bonnie Scotland, can share the joy of their faith today!

"A Person Whom the Light Shines Through"

DURING our four week stay at Pompton Plains in New Jersey, while on a summer pulpit exchange, we met many interesting and gifted people within the congregation there. One such person was Dr. Bea Kettlewood.

Bea was a retired teacher of art and some of her paintings which I was privileged to view were absolutely glorious. Indeed on my final Sunday in the Pompton pulpit I was presented with a painting which depicts their lovely little church in the four seasons — the work of Dr. Bea Kettlewood. I will cherish it always. Even before we had unpacked the suitcases, the painting — which had been lovingly carried across the Atlantic with velvet gloves as "hand luggage" — had been hung in Nairn Old Manse hallway, where it will have pride of place for ever and a day!

Towards the end of our time in Pompton Plains Bea invited Margaret and me to go along with her to see the chapel in the recently opened Chiltern Hospital, not very far from the lovely church in which Bea was a devoted elder. The vision of those who had planned the chapel there was that of a multi-denominational chapel where people of every denomination could reach out to God in their own way. It is very contemporary in its design but it is the most beautiful and peaceful chapel I have ever visited . . . . and the stained glass windows which constituted each of the five walls of the pentagonal building were breathtakingly beautiful! You might not be surprised to learn that these were the work of Bea Kettlewood. The colour and the symbolism in each window was so magnificent that I just had to take colour slides of them so that I could show them in due course to the people of Nairn.

Bea designed five main windows — the window of FAITH, depicting the burning bush to remind us that experiences of life are holy when we recognise the presence of God in them — the window of LIGHT, depicting some of the images of creation to remind us of the "light which shines out of the darkness" — the window of LIFE, representing the tree in the middle of the garden, reminding us that life is a sacred mystery with endless possibilities, and that the gift of life must be nurtured if it is to grow — the window of PEACE, drawing its inspiration from the lovely 23rd Psalm and

Dr. Bea Kettlewood shedding some light on her stained glass window designs.

calling us beyond the stresses and strains of today's life to "green pastures and still waters" — and finally the window of HOPE, depicting the Phoenix rising from the ashes, reminding us that life is filled with experiences of re-birth. (In the picture you can see Bea and Margaret discussing the beautiful stained glass with the window of LIFE in the background).

You won't be surprised to learn that Dr. Bea Kettlewood freely gifted her window designs to her local hospital. "After all," she remarked, "I didn't create them — the ideas just spontaneously came to me — my mind and my hands were clearly being guided by someone else!"

Of course Bea was referring to her own creator, God. And there's no doubt that God most certainly does speak to us through human achievements. It is He who inspires artists, motivates musicians and fires the minds, nerves and hands of scientists and craftsmen . . . . God, the Creator!

There's a lovely story often told which always reminds me of stained glass windows. In the story the question is asked, "What is a saint?" — and the answer which follows is — "A person whom the light shines through."

I shall never again hear that story but think of Dr. Bea Kettlewood over in Pompton Plains. Not only does the light of the creator God gloriously shine through the beautiful stained glass windows she designed for her local hospital chapel, but equally it most surely shines through the one who said with characteristic humility, "I didn't do it!"

The Wheelies are Coming!

AFTER much discussion and procrastination by those concerned at local level . . . . THE WHEELIES ARE COMING! Every householder in the town is to be issued with a new "Wheelie" dustbin. The shops and commercial premises have had them for some time now, but in a few short weeks we'll all be the proud owners of what my friends in the U.S. of A. call their "automated mobile garbage disposal facility" — in other words — their "wheelie bin"!

Full credit to the local council officials for putting the wheels in motion in order to prepare householders for the arrival of their new refuse receptacles. Leaflets on the matter have been delivered to every home and meetings and exhibitions have been arranged at which councillors and council officials, together with representatives from the bin supply company, have been on hand to answer any queries about the new project. Indeed, a sample "wheelie bin" has even been on display outside the Town Hall!

There is no doubt that their introduction will be a vast improvement in terms of refuse collection, and what's more, as far as the local council is concerned, the new system will be much more hygenic to operate AND more environmentally friendly.

Wherever we live — and whatever "garbage disposal facility" is in operation — we really should be tremendously grateful to those responsible for uplifting our rubbish week in week out. Unless they did so, everything would just pile up . . . . the empty tins, bottles, potato peelings, dirt from our vacuum cleaners, uneaten food scraped off our plates, and all the other rubbish that gathers. And of course the longer it would lie, the worse the smell would become! The very thought of piles of untreated rubbish and refuse rotting away by the minute makes us very glad indeed that there are those available to relieve us of it!

Of course it's not just on the outside of us that rubbish can pile up — how quickly all sorts of rubbish can gather within us! Jesus was very conscious of this, and when he warned the people of his day of this danger he was thinking of all the mean and nasty things that can pile up in our minds and in our hearts. Indeed the psalmist, long before the time of Jesus, had spoken about the necessity of being "clean and pure of heart and mind" before entering into God's holy temple.

45

Just think — what a happier place the world would be if each of us could take all of last week's greediness and selfishness and laziness, together with all the disputes and arguments and lies and acts of cruelty, and simply drop them into our "wheelie bin"! They would be whisked away never to be seen again and disposed of — and what's more we could each start afresh.

Of course, this is one of the very reasons why Jesus came to earth so long ago — to take away the sinful rubbish that pollutes our hearts, our minds and and our lives. Indeed, this is why so many people go to church week by week — to get a clean, fresh start . . . . and oh, how we need it!

A Wonderful and Historic Occasion

NAIRN Old Parish Church held recently a truly memorable and historic service to mark the Centenary of the laying of the kirk's Foundation Stone.

The laying of the Foundation Stone.

The stone was laid on 29th August 1894 by Mr. J. A. Grant of Househill, Nairn who was later to become Sir James Augustus Grant. His late father — also J. A. Grant — was a former elder of the town's original Old Parish Church and is remembered to this day as "Grant of the Nile". Together with explorer John Speke in 1860, the father of the man who laid our foundation stone, discovered the source of the River Nile!

Young Mr. Grant was deputising at the very last minute for the County's Lord Lieutenant, The Earl of Leven and Melville who should have laid the stone, but had taken ill. However at the commemorative service 100 years on the present Lord and Lady Leven graced us with their presence and Lord Leven suitably addressed the large congregation who packed the church. Also present was the Moderator of the Presbytery, who was guest preacher and who presented Long Service Certificates to seven of our elders whose joint years of service to the kirk totalled 247 years!

It was a particular joy to have with us for the occasion the two grand-daughters of the Convener of the Building Committee one hundred years ago, Mr. Hugh Mackintosh who played a most significant role in the building of our beautiful church. Indeed one of our stained glass windows was installed in memory of him.

A commemorative Order of Service was prepared and in the course of the special service, as far as possible, we sung the psalms and read the Scripture Lessons used "on the day" 100 years ago. In addition to this we reproduced on the back of the special Order of Service, the original

47

order of events which had fortunately been held in the church's archives. I said to those present that we had done this because they would probably have mislaid their original copy by now!

The ladies responsible for arranging the church flowers for that day truly excelled themselves — the display was absolutely glorious! The blooms were beautifully bedecked around the church's original plan, which was mounted on an easel, and at floor level could be seen two large stones together with some corn, some wine and some oil. Mrs. Burns, the wife of the minister of the day had poured these over the stone after it had been hoisted into place. Additionally the display featured some ancient stonemaking tools together with a rather antique looking spirit level!

When the stone was laid 100 years ago a cylinder was placed within it containing all sorts of memorabilia including, a sovereign, a crown, a four-shilling piece, a three-penny piece, two half-pennies, two farthings, twelve local newspapers, a photograph of the minister, a photograph of the architect, a record of the elders and deacons serving at that time and a record of the Parish Church of Nairn from 1492 — 1894. Of course none of these were unearthed for the occasion — they will remain where they were placed for all time!

It was a truly wonderful and historic occasion and one on which the large congregation of today was enabled to express its thanks for those of yesteryear who had the vision and the enthusiasm to initiate the building of our beautiful Parish Kirk.

But, as I pointed out at the anniversary service, it is the continuing responsibity of the congregation of today to ensure that our handsome church continues to stand where it has stood during the last hundred years for the generations of tomorrow.

Let us never forget that the church buildings which we have all inherited stand as symbols of and as centres for CHRISTIAN WORSHIP and WITNESS in the name and for the sake of the One who is the only SURE FOUNDATION, Jesus Christ, the same yesterday, today and forever, the head and cornerstone of each of our lives.

"Your Sins will Find You Out!"

LOOKING ahead to my next pulpit exchange to the U.S.A. I was searching through my treasure trove of children's stories in order to find one or two that would be equally acceptable with the boys and girls in America as the boys and girls in Scotland had found them. The problem was, which stories would I take with me — there were so many to choose from! Eventually however I drew up a short leet, and the one I'm about to share with you now, I reckoned, just had to be included!

The story concerns SIN — and I included it in my selection because I felt sure that sin would be just as much in vogue in New Jersey as it is here in Bonnie Scotland!

Most stories aimed towards children each have a moral, or a lesson, to them. Sometimes the moral is hidden, and sometimes it is obvious from the very beginning. The moral in the "SIN" story couldn't have been more obvious from the very outset, because it was part and parcel of the story title, namely, in the words of the old cliché — "YOUR SINS WILL FIND YOU OUT!"

It concerned a man in a small town who owned a small corner shop . . . . a grocery-cum-everything kind of shop. On a particular Saturday evening, he had been so busy during the day, that he was practically sold out. All his fruit and vegetables had gone, his fresh bread and his sugar and milk too. Apart from some tins of this and that on his shelves, all he had left to sell was one fresh chicken.

But it was time for shutting up shop, so he locked the front door and turned his notice to read "closed". Then he went to the refrigerated display case under the counter — picked out the remaining chicken and took it through to the large refrigerator in the back shop.

Just then he heard someone knocking rather desperately on his front door — it was a woman whose face he recognised, so he went over and opened it. "Oh, please can you help me," she said, "visitors have just arrived totally unexpectedly and I've nothing to give them for dinner!" "Sure" said the shopkeeper, "would you like a chicken?" "That would do just fine," the woman with relief responded.

Back through to the rear of his shop he went to retrieve the chicken from the fridge. He thereupon weighed it and said to the lady, "That will be £3.65." "Oh," she said, "I rather think I'll need one a bit bigger than that — there will be quite a lot of us for dinner." "Well hang on and I'll see what I have," said the man in the shop lifting the chicken off the scales.

Through to the back shop he went once more, and then you'll never believe what he did! He took the chicken (the same chicken) and he pulled out the wings and the legs a bit to make it look bigger . . . . he stretched it out! Then he returned to the lady, he put it on the scales again — but this time he let his little finger linger on the scales too to make the chicken seem heavier! "That will be £4.85" he said. "Oh, that's better" said the woman, "I'll take them both!"

"YOUR SINS WILL FIND YOU OUT!"

High on a Hill

I recently had occasion to visit the lovely country parish of Ardclach which nestles in the most beautiful Highland countryside not far from my own parish in Nairn.

The Ardclach Bell Tower.

Ardclach has two churches, the first of which was built in 1626 and is situated in a low valley beside the bonnie banks of the River Findhorn. This building is disused now and has been for many years, although the small cemetery surrounding it is still in use. Its successor however, built in 1892 on a much more convenient and accessible site, is still very much in use and morning worship is conducted there Sunday by Sunday.

However some years following the construction of the original country kirk on the left bank of the Findhorn, the Ardclach Bell Tower was built, and it was situated on the crest of a hill high above the old kirk. In fact it is said that this bell tower is the highest of its type in Scotland.

The records show that it was built by a certain Alexander Brodie of Lethen and that the construction served both as a belfry and as a watchtower. Brodie apparently was an ardent Covenanter who had been attacked on several occasions by the royalist faction, and the erection of this tower may possibly have been due to his rather precarious position!

Additionally of course the tower served as a belfry for the parishioners of Ardclach. It would have been totally pointless and quite ridiculous to have rung a church bell in such a low-lying position — where the original church was — and so, by situating it high on the hill, its toll could clearly be heard for miles around summoning the people of the parish to worship.

My visit to the Bell Tower at Ardclach reminded me very cogently of a story which Jesus once told to his disciples. It's contained in St.Matthew's gospel in the passage known as the Sermon on the Mount. Jesus talks there to his friends about setting — not a bell tower — but a CITY — high on a hill. "A city which is situated there," said Jesus, "can never be hidden!"

The point he is clearly making is that Christianity is something which is meant to be seen. A person's faith in Jesus Christ should be visibly apparent in the way in which he lives out his life from day to day . . . . and like the bell high on the hill, that faith should resound and ring out clearly for all to hear!

Saved by a Vision

1994 is truly a celebrationary year — not only is "The People's Friend" notching up its 125th anniversary — so also is the country's second largest children's charity, National Children's Home.

In 1869, sometime during which the gala issue of the "Friend" rolled of the Dundee presses, a young Methodist Minister stepped forward in a very practical way, south of the border, to help the homeless children in London, and in so doing launched N.C.H. as we know it today.

Much of London at that time was squalid and corrupt and countless homeless boys and girls wandered the streets, stealing and begging in order to survive. The sad scene inspired some, like Charles Dickens, to write, but it inspired others to help in a very positive way, not least Rev. Thomas Bowden Stephenson.

Stephenson had a vision. The workhouse (so vividly described by Dickens in "Oliver Twist") seemed the only alternative to life on the streets for many young folks, and so Thomas Stephenson could see that fresh ideas were urgently needed in order to arrest a situation he described as "a little nation of vagrant children living in London's streets". He was inspired to renovate a cottage in Lambeth, near Waterloo Station, with the view to housing initially at least some of the capital's homeless children.

The first two boys, George and Fred, were duly taken in and welcomed on 9th July 1869 and Rev. Stephenson christened his venture, "THE CHILDREN'S HOME". A new social movement to protect youngsters from crime, poverty, neglect, violence and abuse — and a campaign for decent living conditions — was born.

The ensuing six years were significant ones in the development of children's welfare in this country. Stephenson, in establishing his Family System, ensured that boys and girls in care lived within small family groups and were catered for — and loved — by trained staff.

Indeed within two short years of its birth, The Children's Home had expanded into a redundant paving factory in East London. The founder went on to open a country branch on the Moors near Bolton in 1872 and many others quickly followed — Birmingham, Hampshire and the Isle of Man.

NCH Founder, Methodist Minister
Thomas Bowman Stephenson,
with boys from "The Home",
circa 1869.

Thomas Stephenson felt that many of the young children who had been rescued from city destitution and starvation were able to benefit considerably from the fresh and robust life in the country, and so he continued with inordinate enthusiasm to seek and to save more and more lost and destitute young folks from London's streets.

In all his kindly, caring, Christian work, Stephenson was in no way slow to introduce new and innovative ideas, and today 125 years on, N.C.H. is still one of Britain's pioneering childcare charities. Very few of today's pioneering projects are in fact Children's Homes — the emphasis has shifted to developing preventative and support services at centres which concentrate on keeping families together by providing help — through some 200 projects — for 16,000 of the country's most vulnerable children, families and young people.

There are many in "the nineties", both young and not so young alike who have benefited enormously from the Christ-like care and compassion of this childcare charity, and who today have much for which to be grateful. Not least gratitude beyond measure is expressed by all of us I'm sure to its founder, Rev. Thomas Bowden Stephenson and for his vision of 1869.

We read in the Bible these words: "WHERE THERE IS NO VISION, THE PEOPLE PERISH." Without the vision of the founder of N.C.H. many of the nation's vagrant children of yesteryear would most surely have perished as they roamed the streets of London struggling to survive.

And over the years without the care and compassion of this laudable and respected charity, the lives of many children and of their families would have been immeasurably impoverished.

In this 125th anniversary year 1994 — which is also the International Year of the Family — we pray for God's continued blessing on the ongoing pioneering work of N.C.H. and on the children and families they lovingly support today.

The Nairn Connection

I NDEED it's a small world! A few weeks after one of my "Manse Window" articles appeared in print I received a letter from Nairn to Nairn! Let me explain! The letter was written by a male reader of the "Friend", a Mr Alan Nairn of Kettering, and sent to me here at Nairn.

His reason for writing was to enquire if I might know — or could trace — the man who had been his former army training officer during the years of the second world war. Alan had served with the Black Watch Regiment and following his initial "joining up" he was sent to one of the regiment's training camps just outside Perth.

He remembered his training officer well, a certain Corporal Scott and he remembered too that the corporal hailed originally from the town of Nairn — hence Alan's letter to yours truly! In the letter Alan rather amusingly recalled his army training experiences and in particular his memories of training officer Scott. "Any time I didn't quite come up to the mark in terms of what he asked me to do while training," remarked Alan, "the corporal would yell out at the top of his voice: 'NAIRN, YOU'RE A DISGRACE TO YOUR NAME!' "

I'm sure Alan wasn't a disgrace to his surname, but it's understandable that his training officer would readily latch on to the "Nairn" connection and use it in such a tongue in cheek way — it was a gift to him in the situation!

The Wallace Bandstand, Nairn.

55

Following Alan's letter I immediately set out to see if the Cpl. Scott to whom he referred in his letter was related to any of the Scotts on the congregational roll of Nairn Old Parish Church, but to no avail. Not to be beaten however I decided to have a word with the Nairn Old Church Officer, Jack Ferries. Jack too is an old soldier and also a member of the local British Legion Club, and needless to say he was more than willing to engage in a bit of investigation on behalf of an old comrade south of the border.

Within two or three days Jack came back to me with the result we were hoping for. Corporal Scott was alive and well and still lived locally in his beloved Nairn to which he had returned following demobilisation! "Scotty", as he's now known to his friends was absolutely thrilled to learn of the letter — via the "Friend" — with the Nairn connection, and since then Alan Nairn and "Scotty" his former army instructor, out of contact for so long, have been in regular touch. No doubt they have been reminiscing on their days in the Black Watch — and filling in the years since they last met in 1942!

Yes, it's a small world — and it's really amazing the connections we discover from time to time! But there's an even more significant connection that every one of us too often fails to realise. It was Rabbie Burns, Scotland's national bard, who spoke about "man to man the world o'er being brithers" — or brothers.

The Nairn shoreline.

And herein lies the crucial connection! We are all children of the one loving Father . . . . whose name is God — a God and Father who never loses touch with any of his family, and who cares for each one of them more than they could ever know!

(Cpl. Scott has now passed to higher service — we dedicate this story to his memory.)

GRAMPIAN TELEVISION

SOME HOLIDAY "REFLECTIONS"

MONDAY

(Cue Ian at piano . . . . 25 seconds of "Let's get away from it all")

Nice to be with you again! "Let's take a boat to Bermuda, let's take a plane to St. Paul," . . . . the Sinatra evergreen, "Let's get away from it all".

Many of us are doing just that around now and with the help of the Grampian T.V. white grand piano once again, we'll be calling in at quite a few holiday destinations this week!

But most of us feel we do NEED to get away from it all at times . . . . many regard it as necessary. Well, it was absolutely necessary for Jesus Christ, so how much more necessary must it be for you and me? Often we read in the New Testament of Jesus going away to a quiet place in order to recharge, refresh and regenerate himself for the task God had given him to do during his earthly life.

As you and your families "get away from it all" — or even enjoy the break at home this year — may your holiday time be one of relaxation, refreshment and regeneration, that you may return from it revitalised and renewed for the lesser, but none the less important tasks which God has assigned to each one of us. Happy holiday!

(Ian plays out with a further 20 seconds of "Let's get away from it all")

TUESDAY

(Cue Ian at piano . . . . 30 seconds of "New York, New York")

The great showstopper, "New York, New York"! — an increasingly popular holiday venue — and indeed I hope to spend some time once again in the "Big Apple" this year during my pulpit exchange to New Jersey.

The song begins: "Start spreading the NEWS" — you know, that's what this programme "Reflections" is all about — spreading the news, the GOOD news of Jesus Christ, and the Church must take every opportunity the media offers it to engage in the good-news-spreading business.

Communication is the name of the game! I'm a member of the Church of Scotland's BOARD of Communication, which takes in our Press Office, co-operating every day with the news media in the interests of the gospel. And then there's the monthly magazine, "Life and Work" — the St. Andrew Press, the Kirk's own publishing house — and not least "Pathway Productions" the Kirk's own professional T.V. company making programmes for the media in the interests of spreading the news!

So whether you're going to New York, New York, or Newquay or even New Pitsligo or New Elgin . . . . help the church "SPREAD THE NEWS" of the one who promises to make ALL THINGS — INCLUDING OUR LIVES — absolutely NEW! GOODNIGHT!

(Ian plays out with a further 25 seconds of "New York, New York")

WEDNESDAY

(Cue Ian at piano . . . . 30 seconds of "A Nightingale sang in Berkeley Square")

Hello again — "A Nightingale sang in Berkeley Square" — an all-time favourite — as is the capital city of which it reminds us — LONDON . . . . a very popular holiday/tourist venue, at all times of the year, with its many landmarks and places of interest.

There's another song which reminds us of an equally popular capital city — popular and REVERED by the religions of the world. "Jerusalem, Jerusalem, lift up your gates and sing!" The HOLY city Jerusalem is often called . . . . we think, because, as Solomon's Temple had been built there centuries ago, this gave the city a powerful religious appeal. And there are countless biblical landmarks in and around Jerusalem.

But not least, by CHRISTIANITY is this capital city revered . . . . we read of Jesus on several occasions paying it a visit . . . . when he was presented in the Jerusalem Temple by his parents . . . . when he returned there after the Passover Festival . . . . and not least, when he went there for the last time prior to his DESERTION by his disciples and his BETRAYAL by his special friend, Peter.

Oh, there were no nightingales singing in the capital city that night . . . . only cocks crowing. GOODNIGHT.

(Ian plays out with a further 30 seconds of "A Nightingale sang in Berkeley Square")

THURSDAY

(Cue Ian at piano . . . . 35 seconds of "Vienna, city of my dreams")

"Vienna, city of my dreams" — again a very popular holiday destination — truly a city of culture (in addition to Glasgow!) and one which is a MUSICIAN'S dream perhaps. Haydn, Mozart, Beethoven, Schubert, Mahler and Brahms . . . . they all lived in Vienna. But maybe YOUR dreams are focussed on other things . . . . a dream car or a dream house?

Dreams feature frequently in the Bible . . . . young Joseph for example interpreting Pharoah's dreams . . . . many of us have seen the marvellous

"Joseph" musical. But long before that — in the very first book of the Bible in fact — we read of JACOB having a very vivid dream, at a place called Bethel, in which he saw a ladder or a stairway reaching from earth to heaven. Much later on, Jesus referred to Jacob's dream . . . . and in no way is it inappropriate that he did . . . . because isn't that what Jesus personifies? . . . . a "ladder" between earth and heaven . . . . or a stairway . . . . giving man, you and me, constant access to Almighty God!

But as millions throughout the world will testify — this is no dream . . . . it's a reality!

Goodnight.

(Ian plays out with a further 20 seconds of "Vienna, city of my dreams")

FRIDAY

(Cue Ian at piano . . . . 30 seconds of "It's nice to go travellin' ")

I began my "Reflections" with a Sinatra evergreen and I end them on a similar note!

"It's nice to go travellin' to Paris, London or Rome" . . . . in fact, we've been — in song — this week to Bermuda, New York, London and Vienna! Yes, "it's nice to go travellin'" but as the song ends, it's so much nicer to come HOME!

Whether you've BEEN on holiday or are GOING on holiday to Paris, London, or Rome . . . . Stonehaven, Portknockie or perhaps even Nairn (and I can recommend it!) . . . . I do hope you had — or will have — a refreshing time. But it's nice to come home again too!

Perhaps it's the security and love which exists WITHIN our homes and our families that lure us back again. I do hope that these are central to YOUR homes and families. To know that there's someone at home, on hand, to love and to care gives the CHILD an untold sense of security.

Yes, it's nice to go travelling, but as many of us, during this holiday season make tracks for our family home, may we ever remember the UNTOLD sense of security and love which GOD, the Father of all families gives each one of us . . . . and may we ever be aware of his loving presence with us wherever we journey . . . . a presence that transforms our holidays into HOLY-DAYS!

A VERY GOOD AND PEACEFUL NIGHT.

(Ian plays out with a further 30 seconds of "It's nice to go travellin' ")

A Charlie who is Everyone's Darling!

THERE are some people you meet whom you feel, after a very short time, you have known all your life! Such a person was Charlie Flynn (of Irish extraction would you believe!)

Charles and Nina Flynn

Charlie is a youthful looking 88 year old to say the least, and I met him recently in the church in New Jersey where I was on my summer Pulpit Exchange, and also his dear wife Nina whom he wed little more than a year ago! Charlie sadly lost his first wife a few years previously following a happy partnership of over fifty years together, but he found new happiness when he met up with Nina, who was a widow, and after a whirlwind romance the two "youngsters" decided to marry! What a happy and delightful couple they make and they are both committed members of the church there in Pompton Plains, New Jersey!

Charlie is quite a character let me assure you! He's a swimmer par excellence — he swims two to three time a day in his pool in the back garden, and in fact he was diving into his pool with David our son during one of our many visits to his home! One of his boyhood friends was Johnny Weismuller who played the film role of Tarzan. "We both auditioned for the part," said Charlie, "but Weismuller was the best swimmer in our team so he got it!" Another erstwhile friend of Charlie's was a man by the name of Walt Disney! They knew each other well and in their younger days they hung out together in "The Village" (Greenwich Village in New York City) as young commercial artists trying to make a name for themselves. Mr Disney did not too badly of course, but so too did Charlie Flynn —

he has designed the art work and packaging for many products over the years — indeed many of the well known products you can buy in this country have had their packaging and artwork designed by courtesy of Charlie Flynn!

Music plays a large part in Charlie's life — and of course we certainly had that in common! Down in his basement he introduced me to his Player-Piano . . . . which has a story all of its own! Nina's first husband had worked at the docks — he operated a large crane there and one morning he saw something sticking out above the water's surface. He used his crane normally to lift small ships out of the water but on this occasion his crane retrieved a Player Piano which someone had obviously abandoned! He hauled it out, somehow got it home and in the course of time restored it — and now it sounds as good as new! Charlie and Nina have a vast library of scrolls for the piano — everything from "The Blue Danube" to "The bugle boy of company B" to "The Sound of Music". David, Gillian and Jennifer were absolutely intrigued as they had never seen anything like it before!

But the last thing I want to share with you about this remarkable man is his voice . . . . what a marvellous bass voice he has. He sounded like Howard Keel, and he looked a bit like him too come to think of it! He had had some lessons at the famous Juliard Music School in New York City in earlier years, and he sings often in the church both in the choir and as a soloist. "My philosophy is simply this Ian. The good Lord must want me to be here for a purpose — he has given me the voice I've got, so I'm going to continue to use it for as long as I am able to bring some music into the lives of other people . . . . especially the old folks", he quipped!

On the Friday evening before I left the church there in New Jersey for home I organised a concert for the congregation — and guess who I invited to feature in the programme? Charlie sang quite beautifuly and it was a real joy for me to accompany him on the organ. His choice of song was "HOW GREAT THOU ART" and never before have I heard that song sung with so much passion and feeling. There was hardly a dry eye in the church when the song ended. When Charlie sang these words; "Then sings my soul, my Saviour God to thee," he most certainly meant it.

But Charlie's song and his story will go an and on — of that I am sure! And I give thanks that I was able to share so briefly with him in his music and in his story . . . . and I hope you are glad that I shared his story with you!

Two Queen's Men on Parade

A rather historic service took place recently in Nairn Old when one of our B.B. boys was presented with his Queen's Badge, which is the highest award in the Boys' Brigade movement. We are very proud of our B.B. Company, the 1st Nairn, which is the largest in the area with around 130 boys spread over the company's three sections, and as a former B.B. officer myself, I am always delighted when the boys and their officers come to church on parade!

But their recent church parade was very special in that on this occasion Sergeant Andrew Cameron was presented with the B.B.'s ultimate award and became "A Queen's Man".

What made the occasion extra special was that another "Queen's Man" namely Her Majesty's Lord Lieutenant for the County of Nairnshire, The Earl of Leven and Melville was present with us at the service to make the presentation to young Andrew on behalf of Her Majesty. It was particularly appropriate that he be invited to do so, as the Queen is the Patron of the Boys' Brigade movement.

Company Chaplain — Lord Leven, Sgt Andrew Cameron, B.B. Capt. E. Mann

A lovely day was had by all, and it was a proud one. A proud one for Andrew, for the whole B.B. Company, for the congregation of which the company is a vital part, and not least for Andrew's parents and family who were all present to see Lord Leven make the historic presentation towards which Andrew had been working and aiming throughout his boyhood years in the 1st Nairn Company.

In my address to the B.B. boys and the congregation I spoke of another Andrew, the disciple of Jesus who, as many readers will remember, was the one who brought the young lad with the five loaves and two fishes to Jesus. Thanks to disciple Andrew's watchfulness and interest in him, the young lad of Scripture was led to the feet of Jesus, and thanks to the miraculous power Jesus possessed, many were fed with the gifts he brought! The youngster here was the answer to the problem! While it must be admitted that in many instances some young people are the cause of society's problems today, this is not always so — very often the reverse is true — it's just that we don't always hear of these instances.

Christian Youth Organisations of today (and not least the Boys' Brigade) are concerned to bring young people to Jesus Christ, but in order to do so, these young people need others, their seniors and their officers, to take notice of them, to care for them and to lead them.

What a wonderful army of "Andrews" Jesus has gathered around him down through the centuries . . . . Barnardo, Quarrier, Baden Powell of the Boys Scout movement, William Alexander Smith of the B.B. and a host of others, whose representatives in the 1990's are, week in, week out within our churches and our communities seeking out boys and girls and leading them, as Andrew of Scripture did, to the feet of Jesus Christ!

Let us ever acknowledge with gratitude the service of these men and women of dedication and of faith who give so willingly week after week of their time, talents, leadership and love by guiding our lads and our lasses in the ways of Christ and his Kingdom . . . . certainly I know of one young man in Nairn who will be eternally grateful for the leadership that has been so willingly offered to him in the days of his youth — a Queen's Man!

A Faith which no Fire can Destroy

I T was Shakespeare who said that "a little fire is quickly trodden out" — but sometimes alas the fire isn't so little or so easily brought under control.

A few years ago I had the great pleasure of speaking at the Induction of my good friend Rev. Donald Macleod on the occasion of his installation to his first charge, namely the church and parish of Sherbrooke St.Gilbert's in Glasgow.

Donald, as well as being a dedicated minister of the gospel, is a first class musician — he was a violinist in the Ulster Orchestra and then he served in the Scottish National Orchestra for nine years before being called to the ministry. As you may imagine, we have a lot in common and we enjoy making music together whenever we get the opportunity. And so it was a particular honour to be invited to speak on that lovely occasion when he was called to Sherbrooke St. Gilbert's.

Sherbrooke St Gilbert's Church, Glasgow, ablaze.

Never did I think for a minute that in a few short years time all that would be left of that beautiful sanctuary there in the south side of my native city would be charred walls.

But of course accidents happen, and some months ago Donald's lovely church was almost razed to the ground by a terrible fire. I visited the site not long after the tragedy and I just couldn't believe my eyes — all that was left was a burnt-out shell, open to the skies. Pews, pulpit, communion table, font, stained glass windows and not least a very fine pipe organ . . . . all of these things just weren't there — and there was no evidence that they had ever been there.

What's more, the congregation are just about to celebrate their hundredth birthday, but alas emergency arrangements have had to be made so that the planned events and services may take place.

Permission to proceed with the rebuilding of the sanctuary was readily given by the authorities concerned, but in the interim the people of Sherbrooke St. Gilbert's are worshipping in their large hall, which was unaffected by the fire and which has been very tastefully adapted. In point

Cross of yew wood in base of charred wood from hammer beam ceiling.

of fact the hall in which they are now worshipping and in which many of their centenary celebrations will take place was the original church where their forebears worshipped one hundred years ago!

Those who visit the temporary sanctuary will notice as I did the most beautiful wooden cross which stands on their borrowed communion table. The story behind this cross is most interesting and one full of significance for the congregation.

It was fashioned by one of the members, Robin Hodge, who is clearly an expert craftsman. Robin created this lovely cross out of yew wood which stands on a base of charred wood — wood that was part of one of the hammer beams of Sherbrooke St Gilbert's previously much admired Hammer Beam Roof. There is of course much symbolism in Robin's cross, not least in his choice of yew wood. This variety is considered by many to be "sacred" wood because it is often planted and grown within consecrated grounds, cemeteries and church yards for example. However, there is additional significance in that traditionally yew wood is not used for carving or for furniture-making until it is one hundred years old. But further, the piece of wood which Robin selected has a darker grain rising from the hammer beam base suggesting the flames which soared through the sanctuary.

But above all I am sure the symbolism speaks to us of this: Out of the pain and despair of the recent fire, of which the minister and congregation have an ever present reminder in the charred wood . . . . there is the CROSS . . . . the symbol of victory over death, and as my dear minister friend Donald has recently said, "I am sure that this cross will remain part of our church furnishings marking for ever this period in its history and proclaiming the undying faith of its message."

I have no doubt whatsoever that very soon, through the dedicated members of Sherbrooke St. Gilbert's, who are the living stones of the church, the phoenix will rise again from the ashes and the glorious music of the gospel for which that congregation and its minister are reknowned will harmoniously resound once more to the greater glory of God and of his Church — a Church "against which even the gates of hell shall not prevail".

The Three Bears!

PERHAPS you will remember that some time ago I introduced you to Gary — the largest, cuddliest teddy bear imaginable! He's still a great favourite with the Nairn Old congregation let me assure you — and especially so with the children in the Sunday School!

Following Gary's story in the "Friend" a reader in Nuneaton, Mrs Louise Burton, was on holiday in Scotland and having read about Gary, she even made a special effort to come as far north as Nairn in the hope that she might just meet him!

Unfortunately I was away from home when Mrs Burton called, but she met up with one of our lady elders Margaret Taylor who happened to be in the Church at the time when Mrs Burton popped in. Margaret was delighted to show our visitor from south of the border the beautiful sanctuary at Nairn Old, and additionally Mrs Burton got a peek at Gary's special chair! (Apart from the Minister, Gary is the only other one in the church with a reserved seat!)

But Mrs Burton's real treat was still to come! "Would you like to see Gary?" asked Margaret. "Oh, that would just make my day!" gasped Mrs Burton, "but only if it's not too much trouble". "If there's someone in at the Manse, it's no trouble at all," Margaret assured her. Fortunately my wife was at home and she was able to give Margaret the key for the Church Vestry where Gary "hides" between Sunday services!

On seeing the lovable bear Mrs Burton was ecstatic! "You see Mrs Taylor, by sheer coincidence during the very week that Mr Hamilton's story about Gary appeared in "The People's Friend", friends in Nuneaton presented me with Rupert and Richard! I find that they give me tremendous pleasure and company, because I live alone now and my vision is very limited. It's just like having friends with me all the time!"

Rupert and Richard, as you can see from their photograph, are nearly as big as Gary — and every bit as cuddly I'm sure!

Since Mrs Burton's visit to Nairn she has been in touch with me asking me to thank Margaret Taylor for making the introduction to Gary possible, and she further suggests that Gary, Rupert and Richard should become friends! Maybe they could become pen pals and correspond with one another — but I fear their writing would be "bearly" legible! But who knows, it might be possible for the three of them to meet up some day . . . . at a teddy bear's picnic perhaps?

Mrs Burton, I know, like many readers, values dearly the many friendships she shares with those in and around where she lives — and especially she cherishes her new found friends, Rupert and Richard!

And there are countless folks like Mrs Burton who now live alone and who appreciate more than anything else, a bit of company, the company of their friends. It's very often the best medicine that could be prescribed for them! As was written long ago in the book of Ecclesiasticus: "A faithful friend is the medicine of life".

And it's a medicine that those of us who are fit and able can readily dispense, if only we would take the time to do so more often! As someone once said, "The only way to have a friend is to be one" and as the words of the one-time popular song remind us:

"WHEN YOU'VE GOT FRIENDS AND NEIGHBOURS, YOU'RE THE RICHEST MAN IN TOWN!"

Look — No Hands!

NOT long ago, thanks to a generous legacy that a late and dear member had left to her beloved parish kirk, our finance committee decided to purchase an electronic piano-organ for use in our newly created Session Room — where most of the church meetings are held.

The lady concerned, who had passed to her Lord's nearer presence, was known, during her lifetime of service to her church, to have a great love of hymn-singing. She was such a dear and kindly soul who had told me often of how much she appreciated the singing of our large Church Choir Sunday by Sunday, and especially the Anthem at morning service. It was felt therefore singularly appropriate that an electronic keyboard, to accompany the hymn-singing in our new Session Room, would be a most fitting purchase and would serve as a most appropriate memorial to a greatly respected member of the congregation, now gone from us — one, let it be said, very much young at heart and with an infectious sense of humour!

The instrument was duly purchased and installed in the Session Room just in time for our monthly meeting of the elders — on the very afternoon of the meeting in fact!

It immediately occurred to the Minister (i.e. yours truly!) how nice it would be to begin the meeting by singing one of the old Scottish metrical Psalms — to the accompaniment of our new keyboard. But it was so late in the day that I just hadn't time to arrange for anyone to play the keyboard at the meeting, far less give anyone the opportunity to familiarise himself with all the push-buttons and switches!

Not to be beaten however I soon realised that the instrument had a recording facility on it, which meant that the required music could be pre-recorded, and then, at the touch of a button, could be played on cue to accompany the singing later that night. So I set to it and played the psalm-tune myself — all seven verses — and stored it in the keyboard's memory in good time for the start of the elders' meeting.

Of course, I couldn't play at the meeting myself because I was "in the chair" leading the opening devotions from the front, but I thought I had "cracked it" as they say, by pre-recording the psalm. All I had to do now was to prime one of the elders with the practicalities of pushing the right button at the right time — which he did!

However the other elders, quite unaware at that early stage of the built-in automatic features of our new keyboard, fully expected someone to PLAY the instrument when I announced the opening psalm! Looking out from behind the table (when the music started to play) was a sight to behold let me assure you! The elders were dumbfounded on hearing the keyboard begin to play the opening psalm, albeit there was no-one sitting on the piano stool! In truth, they just couldn't keep the smile off their faces and it took us until at least the middle of verse two of the psalm to regain our composure! I was tempted at one stage to shout out — "Look — no hands!" — however I refrained!

But there's more! At the end of verse seven, when the elder leaned over to switch the keyboard off, he inadvertently pushed the wrong button and instead of silence we were immediately thereupon treated to the instrument's "demo" tape . . . . which blurted out a deafening up-tempo version of "Eine Kleine Nachtmusik!"

Never, I am sure, in our kirk's one hundred year history has a meeting of the elders got off to a more hilarious start! And I have no doubt whatsoever that there was much laughter in heaven too — not least from dear Margaret with whom the keyboard will be forever lovingly associated!

A Proud, Happy Family Occasion

ALL mums and dads take justifiable pride in the achievements of their offsprings and Margaret and I are no exception let me assure you! Recently we had the pleasure of seeing David being presented with his Boys' Brigade President's Badge at a special service held in Nairn Old Parish Church which I had the privilege of conducting as Chaplain to the 1st Nairn Company.

Margaret, Ian, David, Gillian and Jennifer.

Regular readers of the "Friend" will know how much the Boys' Brigade movement means to myself and to my family. My father, like many, has given a lifetime of faithful service to this great organisation for boys, having served as Captain of two companies in Glasgow, where the movement had its birth. I too, like countless others, have served in the organisation both as boy and as an officer, and indeed I have no doubt at all that it was the B.B. that led me into the full time service of the church and of the Master.

The B.B. was founded on 4th October 1883 by Sir William A. Smith at a mission hall in Glasgow's North Woodside Road. Indeed today you can see a plaque on the wall of the former mission hall building to commemorate the founding of the great movement.

71

William Smith had been born in Thurso but at the age of fifteen he had come south to work in his uncle's shop. In time he became a successful Glasgow businessman himself and also a part-time soldier, but not least he was a faithful churchman. He served as a Sunday School teacher and it was here, due probably to his army interest, that he suddenly came up with his idea of a military styled organisation for the young boys of the city. The older boys in his Sunday School class were rather bored and restless. It was difficult to hold their attention and to keep them under control, but then he hit on the idea of drill and discipline firmly linked to religious instruction, and The Boys' Brigade was born!

The aim and object (as every B.B. boys well knows!) is "the advancement of Christ's kingdom among boys and the promotion of habits of obedience, reverence, discipline, self-respect and all that tends towards a true Christian manliness". Within a year of its founding the boys of the 1st Glasgow Company were in uniform, the traditional cap, belt and haversack, and the B.B. in fact was the first of all the uniformed organisations, which today spreads throughout the world.

Although I am now no longer able to serve as an officer in the B.B. I try to take as active an interest as I can in their work in my role as a Company Chaplain, and I am always delighted when the B.B. are on church parade! We are very fortunate to have here in Nairn one of the Brigade's largest companies in the area, and I have no doubt whatsoever that this is due in no small measure to the devoted men and women who week by week freely give of their time and abilities to lead the boys in the advancement of Christ's kingdom. Between the three sections, Anchor Boys, Junior Section and Company Section, we have around 130 boys on the Company Roll and as a proud parent I am so glad that David is one of them!

Indeed the parents of all three boys in the 1st Nairn were as proud as peacocks when the President of Inverness and District Battalion came along to that special service recently to present Corporals Graham Milne, Donald MacLeod and David Hamilton with their President's Badges! It was truly a happy family occasion for the Milnes, the MacLeods and the Hamiltons, but it was a proud and happy family occasion for the good folks of Nairn Old Parish Church also as our B.B. Company is a very important branch of the family of our congregation.

"Sing Early for Christmas!"

P ART of our summer holiday this year was spent in Scarborough down in Yorkshire — a favourite Hamilton holiday haunt! For over twenty-five years or so Margaret and I have spent many happy hours there and especially at Scarborough's Spa where the tradition of music-making goes back much further than twenty-five years!

Concerts are held there almost daily right throughout the summer months, in the Spa Suncourt Enclosure in the morning and in the magnificent Victorian Spa Grand Hall each evening. Many "Friend" readers will recall I'm sure listening to some glorious music presented and played by the late Max Jaffa and his orchestra over a period of twenty seven seasons at the Spa. Indeed a beautiful memorial plaque situated within the Spa complex marks Max's momentous contribution to music-making over all these years and rightly describes him as "A true musical ambassador for Scarborough".

I still have here in the manse countless programmes from Max Jaffa's Spa concerts and while looking at them recently I discovered one that the maestro himself had autographed for me!

Happily the tradition continues and today a small ten-piece orchestra made up of musicians from many of the country's finest orchestras perform daily a summer serenade to suit every musical palate. Their repertoire is extensive to say the least and includes popular classics, songs from the shows and many old favourites.

At one particular evening concert Margaret and I attended, we were delighted to see on the programme a selection of Bing Crosby songs. However, just before the orchestra started to play it the presenter, who is also a very able and delightful pianist thought that he should tell us that one particular Bing Crosby song — the most famous by far — had not for some reason been included by the arranger of the music. The song of course was "White Christmas." "So let's all sing it and get it out of our system" said Simon, "and then we'll launch into the others!"

The Suncourt Enclosure, Scarborough.

So there we were sitting singing — on the evening of Sunday 23rd July, one of the hottest days of the month — "I'm dreaming of a White Christmas"!

At first it all seemed just a wee bit incongruous, as well as unseasonal, but when I started to think about it I began to realise that the Christmas seasonal song wasn't really so inappropriate after all.

You see, although we celebrate Christmas, the birth of our Saviour, in December, there's a very real sense in which Jesus is born to many people right throughout the year. Wherever and whenever men and women and boys and girls first hear about Jesus and his great love for them, in a sense it's Christmas! Jesus is born in their hearts and in their lives and what a wonderful day that must be for them. Oh, there are no wise men, no shepherds, no angels, no star, no manger, no gold, frankincense or myrrh, no sleighbells ringing, no snowflakes glistening — and certainly no seasonal songs like "White Christmas"!

But day in, day out, somewhere in this vast world Jesus Christ is born to someone. Isn't it a wonderful thought that for someone, somewhere, ANY day of ANY month of ANY year can be Christmas day?

With these thoughts in mind I returned to singing Bing's song down there in the Spa — in July — with the greatest of gusto!

74

A Holiday Encounter with a "Friend"!

D URING a recent short family holiday to the Mediterranean island of Majorca, we decided one afternoon to explore the northern part of this Spanish island, and in particular to visit the small, rather exquisite beach at Formentor — known as the millionaire's paradise!

It's said that the great composer Chopin — who is one of my favourites — spent the winter of 1838/39 on Majorca and that he composed some of his finest Preludes and Nocturnes at a place called Valldemosa on the west of the island, but it is recorded that Chopin also visited Formentor in the north — where we were. If the great man was alive today I have no doubt whatsoever that he too would be a millionaire on the royalties from on his beautiful music, music that has travelled the length and breadth of the world.

I didn't meet many millionaires on my trip to Formentor let me say, but I did have the most unbelievable encounter with a rather special "Friend"! Let me explain!

When we sat down on the wall around Formentor's most exclusive beach we discovered — lying on the wall — some reading material which someone had obviously left behind. There was a newspaper and a magazine. I can't honestly remember what newspaper it was, but the magazine — lying there on the beach wall at Formentor in northern Majorca — was "THE PEOPLE'S FRIEND"! I could hardly believe my eyes when I saw it lying there — and I can even tell you who it belonged to, because the owner's name was written on the top right hand corner — "Thomson" (Any relation to "D.C." I wonder!)

"Open it up dad and see if you're in it" said the twins, and when I did so I discovered in fact that the "Manse Window" feature was NOT mine in this edition, but that of my good friend Dr. James Martin. But at the end of Jim's story was printed: "NEXT WEEK, THE REV. IAN HAMILTON WONDERS WHAT TO DO!" I certainly had no hesitation about what to do following the holiday encounter with my "Friend"! "Margaret — you must get a photograph of this, I'm sure there's a future "Manse Window" story in it somewhere!"

Indeed, it's a story of co-incidences. What a co-incidence for a Church of Scotland minister to discover in that small and relatively quiet part of the Island of Majorca a copy of this magazine with which he is privileged to be associated! And what a co-incidence that Dr. Jim Martin's "Manse Window" story was about the Church of Scotland School at Tabeetha in Jaffa — also on the shores of the Mediterranean — albeit quite a bit upstream! And what a co-incidence to discover that one of my favourite composers had written so much of the music I love to play in and around this part of Majorca!

Not only does Chopin's music beautiful music go around the world, but so too, it appears, does "THE PEOPLE'S FRIEND"! And with it goes these "Manse Window" messages that myself and my fellow-contributors regularly write, through which we try to help spread — to every continent and island — the good news of the One who once lived and worked and walked not very far from these Mediterranean shores.

He of course is the most perfect Friend of all, and to encounter Him — wherever — is a more wonderful experience by far!

GRAMPIAN TELEVISION

SOME FINAL "REFLECTIONS"

MONDAY

(Cue Ian at piano . . . . 30 seconds from "A Little Night Music")

Nice to be with you again . . . . a little excerpt there from "A Little Night Music" . . . . and now I'd like to share with you a little story which I once read, concerning a little man by the name of "Little". Mr Little had a charming little wife, and there were quite a few little Littles.

But alas Mr Little had only a little money, so he and his little wife and the little Littles had somehow to make a little go a long, long way.

Their neighbours wondered how on earth Mr and Mrs Little could be so happy on such a little . . . . so eventually someone put it TO Mr Little, "Mr Little, how do you and Mrs Little and all the little Littles manage on such a little?" "Oh," replied Mr Little with a broad smile on his face, "we manage just fine on very little . . . . because you see, EVERY LITTLE HELPS!"

Enjoy the little that's left of today and I'll see you again, for a little, tomorrow!

(Ian plays out with a further 30 seconds of "A Little Night Music")

TUESDAY

(Cue Ian at piano . . . . 25 seconds of "Make me a channel of your peace")

"Make me a channel of your peace" — the words of the famous prayer attributed to St. Francis of Assisi transposed into song.

The story is told that, one day St. Francis said to a young monk, "Brother, let us go down into town today, and PREACH". And so off they set exchanging conversation as they walked along.

Through the busy streets and narrow alleys . . . . right to the edge of the town, and even to the village beyond they journeyed . . . . and eventually they arrived back at the monastery. As they were passing through the high gates the young cleric turned to his senior and asked "Father, when are we going to preach?"

"My child," said St. Francis, "we HAVE been preaching . . . . we were preaching while we were walking. We have been seen, looked at, our behaviour has been noticed, people have remarked . . . . and so we have delivered a morning sermon. You see my son, there is no point in walking anywhere to preach, unless we PREACH as we WALK."

(Ian plays out with a further 25 seconds of "Make me a channel of your peace")

WEDNESDAY

(Cue Ian at piano . . . . 20 seconds of "Scarborough Fair")

Hello again. A favourite holiday spot of ours is Scarborough in Yorkshire. We have many happy memories of family holidays spent down there, and especially of the orchestral concerts in Scarborough's Spa Grand Hall, presented for twenty seven seasons by the late and legendary Max Jaffa.

Those of you who know the popular resort will be familiar with the pier fairground at the foot of the castle cliff, beside the harbour.

Two young girls were enjoying all the fun of the SCARBOROUGH Fair — not least a bump about on the ever-popular dodgems! But as they happily drove around the track they both suddenly caught sight of a small boy standing on the perimeter deck looking on.

The lad was on his own, he looked a bit shabby and he had obviously been crying. As soon as their time was up the girls went over to the small boy to ask what was wrong.

"I had fifty pence for a ride on the dodgems" he explained, "but when I went to get it out of my pocket it dropped through one of these spaces on the pier and down into the water."

"Jump into a car!" ordered one of the girls, "it's our shout . . . . and we'll wave to you as you go round!" So round and round the wee boy went, his face beaming . . . . and after one go, the girls stood him a second!

Later in the day when reminiscing on their visit to Scarborough Fair, the one girl said to the other, "You know, I enjoyed the goes we DIDN'T have best of all!"

"IT IS MORE BLESSED TO GIVE THAN TO RECEIVE."

(Ian plays out with a further 20 seconds of "Scarborough Fair")

THURSDAY

(Cue Ian at piano . . . . 20 seconds of "Schubert's Serenade")

A beautiful melody — "Schubert's Serenade" — and incidentally this music was the late Max Jaffa's signature tune at his concerts in the Spa Grand Hall, Scarborough to which I was referring last night.

Schubert is among the "greats" in terms of composers . . . . although he never lived to know it. His beginnings were so humble and his early life so poor that at times he didn't even have the money to buy the paper on which to write his "masterpieces of tomorrow".

One day Schubert and a few friends were in a Viennese tavern — talking and drinking — the last place on earth in which to compose music! The clanking of mugs and the babble of voices was half-deafening!

But in the middle of it all Schubert sat glancing over some poems a friend had given him. "I've a lovely melody in my head," he suddenly exclaimed, "and I could put it down if only I had paper with some lines on it."

78

A friend grabbed a menu from a neighbouring table, quickly ruled some lines on the back of it and handed it to Schubert. The babble and the clanking and the laughing went on.

But there in the midst of it all was born that passionate, imperishable melody, "Schubert's Serenade" . . . . one that will live forever, from the pen of an all-time "great".

History is full of people who rose from the humblest of beginnings to TRUE GREATNESS . . . . and indeed in the GOD of HISTORY is this concept PERSONIFIED to perfection!

(Ian plays out with a further 20 seconds of "Schubert's Serenade")

FRIDAY

(Cue Ian at piano . . . . 30 seconds of "Stranger on the Shore")

"Stranger on the Shore" by Acker Bilk . . . . a "sixties" number, and still very popular in the nineties!

There's a lovely Bible story about a stranger on the shore — the incident happened after the resurrection of Jesus.

Some of his friends had gone back to their old jobs, like fishing, and one night they set sail as usual on the Sea of Galilee . . . . but to no avail, not one single fish did they catch!

At daybreak someone from the shore shouted out to them to cast their nets on the other side of their boat. This they did, and almost immediately these nets were amazingly full and running over!

It was at this point that they realised who the Stranger on the shore was . . . . and what a special morning that turned out to be for these men! In fact, the whole experience turned their lives upside down!

And THAT version of "Stranger on the Shore" goes back to the sixties too . . . . no, not to the "swinging" sixties — but rather IT relates to an incident that would have been on the lips of the early Christian community probably around A.D.60! . . . . and even before that!

This "STRANGER ON THE SHORE" will live forever!

(Ian plays out with a further 30 seconds of "Stranger on the Shore")

79

AND FINALLY . . . .
"The Day the *Minister* made the Wrong Choice!"

MANY of you may remember a story I had published some time ago concerning a certain youngster in our Sunday School and the reply he gave me to a question I asked from the pulpit one Sunday.

I had been telling the boys and girls that I had got no answer when I had called to visit Mrs Anderson. Next day I met her in the High Street and she immediately apologised that she had been out when I had called. "How did Mrs Anderson know that I had been at her door?" boys and girls. I had fully expected a reply along the lines of a visiting card popped through the letterbox by the Minister.

But then I should have known better! The wee chap's response to the question was as follows: "She was hiding behind the curtain!" People still comment to me on that story wherever I go, and indeed sometimes they even ask me how my young friend is doing! Well, he's as large as life let me assure you AND he now has a partner in crime it would seem!

The boys and girls have been recently doing in Sunday School a series of lessons on "choices" so I thought that on a particular Sunday I would complement the series in Church with the children before they left for their classes.

"Which of these would you choose boys and girls," I asked, "a brand new mountain bike, or a luxury holiday abroad in the sunshine?" Hands galore went up and I gave young Carol the opportunity to tell the congregation what her preference would be. The choice between the two was quite difficult to make but after a bit of thought she went for the mountain bike!

"Which of **these** two would you prefer boys and girls — an evening spent at a pop concert to hear your favourite band or group, or an evening spent doing an extra dose of homework?" "The pop concert," Jayne responded without a second's hesitation needless to say! (To which the remaining 50-60 children said "Amen" . . . . well, it WAS an easier choice!)

"A final choice for you boys and girls" I continued. "Which of THESE would you choose?" In the one hand I held up a box of mouth-watering plain and milk chocolates, an in the other a bottle clearly marked "CASTOR OIL"! Again, hands went up galore, and I had to choose someone else to reply. "Yes Simon, which of these would you prefer, a lovely box of chocs or a dose of castor oil?" "THE CASTOR OIL" he bellowed forth!

80

The congregation were helpless laughing — especially when, after realising the error of MY choice, I went on to say: "OK then Simon — you can have it, and if you come up to the pulpit on your way to Sunday School shortly I'll be happy to give you a good spoonful myself!"

When the hilarity eventually died down and we all regained a measure of composure I went on to teach the boys and girls about the serious business of having to make choices in the course of our lives.

At a young age, little ones have choices to make — what games to play — where to play — whom to play with. As they get older and move up from Primary school to Secondary school they find more and more choices being put before them like, what subjects to study, or what organisations or clubs to join? When they become young adults, other and more demanding choices present themselves like, What will I do with my life? — How will I prepare for that? — Where is the best place to get the training I need?

But the most important choice which every one of us must make, whatever our age, concerns the purpose to which we will devote our life. And, as I explained to the boys and girls in the Sunday School, countless millions of people throughout the world have chosen to follow Jesus Christ and to devote their lives to the up-building of his church so that more and more people may learn of his love for them.

"There's no doubt boys and girls that life in God's service is the best possible choice anyone can make, and making that choice involves coming to church and to Sunday School to worship and praise God week by week, AND by learning love and to forgive one another as Jesus loves and forgives each one of us."

After the service during coffee time the topic on everyone's lips of course was the Minister's choice of the Castor Oil Kid! "Don't worry Ian," said one of the elders patting me on the shoulder, "the story for the children today was absolutely Bible-based . . . . Jesus chose a Simon too!"

PIANO CASSETTE OFFER

Rev. IAN HAMILTON'S

piano serenade

SIDE 1		SIDE 2	
Serenade (Schubert)	*arr. Hamilton*	To Music	*Schubert*
Viennese Whirl	*arr. Hamilton*	Nightingale in Berkeley Square	*arr. Hamilton*
Embraceable You	*George Gershwin*	Gillian and Jennifer	*Hamilton*
Largo	*Handel*	The Songs of Ivor Novello	*arr. Hamilton*
Forgotten Dreams	*Leroy Anderson*	Waltz in A Flat	*Chopin*
Prelude in E Minor	*Chopin*	All The Things You Are	*Jerome Kern*

Available by post — send **£6.50** *(including P&P)* to:

Piano Cassette Offer, 3 Manse Road, Nairn IV12 4RN

VIOLIN-PIANO-ORGAN CASSETTE OFFER

"STOPS & STRINGS"

Rev. IAN HAMILTON
PIANO-ORGAN

Rev. DONALD MACLEOD
VIOLIN

SIDE A	
Espana Waltz	*Waldteufel*
In a Monastery Garden — Ketelby	*arr. Hamilton*
Cradle Song	*J. Scott Skinner*
Autumn	*Chaminade*
Adagio — Violin Concerto	*Haydn*
Londonderry Air	*arr. H. Tolhurst*
Liebesleid	*Fritz Kreisler*

SIDE B	
Chanson de Matin	*Elgar*
Andante — Trumpet Concerto — Haydn	*arr. Lloyd Webber*
Fiddle Music Selection	*Traditional*
Sanctuary of the Heart — Keltebey	*arr. Hamilton*
Czardas	*Monti*

Available by post — send **£6.50** *(including P&P)* to:

Violin-Piano-Organ Cassette Offer, 3 Manse Road, Nairn IV12 4RN

VIOLIN-PIANO CASSETTE OFFER

The
"SINGING STRINGS"
of

DONALD MACLEOD
VIOLIN
and
IAN HAMILTON
PIANO

SIDE 1
A Burns Croon
Schon Rosmarin
A Viennese Whirl
Sicilienne
Cavatina

SIDE 2
Entr'acte Gavotte — Mignon
Shetland Fiddle Music
How Wonderful to Know
Canto Amoroso
Gypsy Carnival

Available by post — send **£6.50** *(including P&P) to:*
Violin-Piano Cassette Offer, 3 Manse Road, Nairn IV12 4RN